SHAMANIC CREATIVITY

"Evelyn Rysdyk is a brilliant shamanic teacher who has helped to pioneer shamanic teachings in our time. She knows how to take some of the deeper ancient cross-cultural mysteries and share them with a modern Western culture. Evelyn performed her 'magic' again with *Shamanic Creativity*. This practical guide contains the support, inspiration, clear communication, and shamanic guidance you need to tap into the deepest level of your creativity. This is such a timely book as we all need to own our destiny to create our highest dreams."

SANDRA INGERMAN, MA, AUTHOR OF *WALKING IN LIGHT*
AND COAUTHOR OF *SPEAKING WITH NATURE*

"Kudos to Evelyn Rysdyk's new book *Shamanic Creativity*. This overdue and inspiring book offers in simple language the tools to free old energy blocks, patterns, and ways of thinking to manifest a creative and fulfilling life beyond your expectations. Read it and follow the rituals, energy work, and spirit journeys. It's a must, not just for those who practice shamanism but for anyone who wishes to rediscover and ignite their birthright's life passion."

ITZHAK BEERY, AUTHOR OF *THE GIFT OF SHAMANISM*,
SHAMANIC TRANSFORMATIONS, AND *SHAMANIC HEALING*

"In this moment when we dearly need to access the full range of our wild-hearted creativity, Evelyn Rysdyk offers us a way to do just that. *Shamanic Creativity* is not just for those who identify as 'creatives' but for all of us to discover how we unleash our creative superpower. We are creating the path as we walk it, and we need to course correct. Evelyn offers direct, accessible practices to awaken our slumbering creative potential to be that course correction now, to offer unique new solutions, ingenious risks, and heartfelt weaving of it all together. With the shamanic practices offered and the hope Evelyn inspires, we might just innovate our way into a future that supports the insanely, improbable, fragile, beautiful reality of life on Earth."

CHRISTINA LEE PRATT, FOUNDER OF LAST MASK CENTER

"As a teacher of sacred art I often tell my students that our own life is the greatest piece of art we ever make! We are all part of creation, and it is through our own creations (in the widest possible sense of the word) that we express the innate and divine force within us. Creativity unlocks, heals, and supports wholeness. Evelyn Rysdyk's new book presents a map and 'creative cardinal rules.' Ultimately, she tells us how to transcend conflict and contradiction, view those as fertile ground for new insights and projects, and, in her own words, arrive at *homospatial thinking*. Treat yourself and get started today!"

IMELDA ALMQVIST, AUTHOR OF *SACRED ART* AND
MEDICINE OF THE IMAGINATION

"The ideas and suggestions offered in *Shamanic Creativity* are interesting, inspirational, and supportive for anyone wanting to connect with the creative forces of the universe as well as their own. Evelyn Rysdyk is the epitome of shamanic creativity and a great guide."

MAMA DONNA HENES, URBAN SHAMAN AND
AUTHOR OF *BLESS THIS HOUSE*

"Once again Evelyn Rysdyk shares her deep understanding of shamanic practice coupled with her lifelong experience as a creative artist. You can trust her, as both shaman and artist, to guide your own creative energies into life patterns that will bring greater harmony and empowerment to your everyday life. It will be a joyous journey!"

TOM COWAN, AUTHOR OF *FIRE IN THE HEAD* AND
YEARNING FOR THE WIND

"Creative energy is our birthright. It is life itself speaking through us. In *Shamanic Creativity,* acclaimed author and experienced guide Evelyn C. Rysdyk teaches us how to connect with this limitless vitality, removing the blockages and allowing it to flow unimpeded."

HILLARY S. WEBB, PH.D., AUTHOR OF *YANANTIN AND
MASINTIN IN THE ANDEAN WORLD*

SHAMANIC CREATIVITY

Free the Imagination with Rituals, Energy Work, and Spirit Journeying

EVELYN C. RYSDYK

Destiny Books
Rochester, Vermont

Destiny Books
One Park Street
Rochester, Vermont 05767
www.DestinyBooks.com

Text stock is SFI certified

Destiny Books is a division of Inner Traditions International

Cataloging-in-Publication Data for this title is available from the Library of Congress

ISBN 978-1-64411-354-7 (print)
ISBN 978-1-64411-355-4 (ebook)

Printed and bound in the United States by Lake Book Manufacturing, Inc.
The text stock is SFI certified. The Sustainable Forestry Initiative® program
promotes sustainable forest management.

10 9 8 7 6 5 4 3 2 1

Text design by Priscilla Baker and layout by Virginia Scott Bowman
This book was typeset in Garamond Premier Pro with Winery used as the display
typeface
Illustrations on pages 26, 34, 41, 44, 49, 61, 92, and 95 from Adobe Stock; pages 29,
195, and 197 from Unsplash; pages 69, 85, and 156 from Dreamstime; pages 199
and 200 from Pixabay

To send correspondence to the author of this book, mail a first-class letter to the
author c/o Inner Traditions • Bear & Company, One Park Street, Rochester, VT
05767, and we will forward the communication.

✴

Shamanic Creativity *is dedicated to* you, *no matter where you think you belong on the creativity spectrum.*

You might be a complete creative novice looking to find a new way out of your anxiety, or you might be one of those folks who sidelined your creative pursuits because you felt your efforts weren't as good as someone else's. Last, you might be a self-identified creative looking to open up more of your capabilities.

Wherever you are on that creative energy spectrum, I know that awakening and encouraging your unique and extraordinary genius is a part of transforming the minds and hearts of our collective. Creative energy is a life-giving force that unbinds our imagination, supports our capacity for brilliant innovation, and aids in the implementation of unique, new solutions. These are just the skills we need to open up, amplify, and manifest real, concrete solutions for these perilous times.

Of course, I didn't bring this book into your hands by myself. I want to offer my gratitude to my personal team members: Stephany Evans of Ayesha Pande Literary, Ehud Sperling and Jon Graham at Inner Traditions International for choosing to publish this book, and my partner in all creative adventures, Allie Knowlton.

Contents

INTRODUCTION

The Power of Creative Energy

To be an aware person at this moment in time means experiencing feelings of despair, stress, and anxiety about the wider world. It seems that everywhere you turn, ever scarier news about rising ocean levels, multiyear droughts, wildfires, melting glaciers, extreme weather, and unique new diseases dominates the headlines. The overwhelming, environmentally induced aspect of our collective distress has even been given a name: *solastalgia*.

All of us are suffering from this collective disorder, and our situation feels immense, overwhelming, and profoundly frightening. The effects can be isolating, giving you the feeling that you're having to face the insurmountable alone or that, no matter what you do, your efforts won't make a difference. Our current state of despair limits what solutions we can conceive. While we are in such a state, we simply cannot break through to the imaginative level of uniquely ingenious thinking that this time requires.

But there *is* hope.

To a shaman, everything is primarily energetic in nature. Energy is the armature on which physical reality is formed. In shamanic terms, even the animating essence that we may call spirit or consciousness is part of that energetic landscape. This is the arena in which the shaman is master.

When any imbalance or illness occurs, it means that spiritual energy has fallen out of harmony. Indeed, a shaman's work is primarily focused on the creation and maintenance of energetic harmony and balance. This might entail encouraging harmony and balance in a person for purposes of healing, among people in a local group to maintain tribal harmony, between different groups of people to negotiate harmony and preserve peace, and between people and the surrounding landscape to maintain a healthy environment in which all may flourish.

In their work, shamans strive to increase that which is beneficial and to reduce that which is harmful, to return a healthy state of equilibrium.

Shamans also understand that by attending to the harmony and balance *inside* yourself, you are simultaneously engaged in transforming the entirety. It is why shamanic healers spend the lion's share of their day attending to keeping balance and harmony inside their own lives. They have always understood what the new physics has postulated, which is that our universe functions like a hologram. In other words, even the smallest part of the whole holds all the information of the entirety. The microcosm of your self is both a manifestation of and a doorway to the macrocosm of All That Is.

The destructive illness from which our human community suffers requires healing in a similar manner. While all of nature is engaged in an ongoing cycle of creation and destruction, it's clear that life's energetic balance is now weighted far too heavily to the latter. We need to encourage and increase creative energy to balance our human collective's destructive energy. In so doing, we will heal ourselves and our world.

Nature's creative energy is what continually shapes and reshapes life so that it endures in the face of any circumstance or challenge. It gives a tree the ability to heave up a roadway with its roots, an endangered polar bear the ability to alter its ice-hunting methods so that it can hunt whales, and you and I the ability to find solutions when confronted with a problem. From the evolution that has occurred over many millennia to each year's magical springtime renewal, creative energy is what produces life's continuance.

As a product of nature's creativity, you were also born to be a cre-

Balance within contributes to balance without. This is the shaman's understanding of the cosmos.
(Digital collage of Andromeda Galaxy/NASA © 2012 and 2020 by Evelyn C. Rysdyk)

ator. As such, you were meant to engage with the creative energy that was wired into you as part of your birthright. The world needs all of us to reawaken our brilliant and uniquely ingenious creative minds. That's why I wrote this book.

Everyone's creativity is being called forth to shift our collective into one that is willing to sustain and encourage life. The need for creative thinking and action is especially acute these days, faced as humanity is with climate change and other global challenges. In 1962 the British historian Arnold Toynbee recognized how crucial creativity is socially, noting that "to give a fair chance to potential creativity is a matter of life and death for any society."[1]

Integrating the forces of ordered structure and creative flow is a necessary process for healthy organisms and ecosystems. In a living body, the extremity of order produces death. Life must continue to evolve, change, and move. Stasis has no place. When native organisms are eradicated or replaced through human intervention to create more orderly landscapes, the ecosystem can collapse. On the other hand, unhampered growth of one single organism can be just as deadly.

Certainly, forces are continuing their destruction of our planet. Those forces have reshaped Earth for profit-focused motives perpetrated in the arrogant belief that the linear human mind is in some way capable of altering the exquisite balance of nature so that it serves a small group of humans at the expense of other life-forms. However, since our planetary ecology is an intricately organized closed system of living beings, there truly is no aspect that can be injured or removed without causing damage to the whole.

It's the delicate balance between order and chaos that creates the sweet spot for life.

Inside us, we have the same opposing energies. We have the forces of order, which encompass our linear mind, our domesticated enculturation, the suppression of emotion, our desire for control and fear of losing it, and our desire for predictability. We also have our own inner wildness, the part of us that suffocates when confined to a box. This is what we need to restore and encourage. It is our nonlinear and unbound primal creative energy, our emotions and our physicality, that are being called forth. Embracing the fullness of our being is part of being a creative person and that which can give birth to new, remarkable solutions for our world. We have never needed out-of-the-box holistic thinking and actions more than we do now. That is exactly where creativity can make all the difference.

Since you and I are part of a larger collective, the personal shifts and changes we make create ripples that can alter the whole. Peter Russell, a fellow of the Institute of Noetic Sciences and author of several books, including *The Global Brain Awakens, The Consciousness Revolution,* and *From Science to God,* shared a formula for large-scale transformation. He proposed that any shift occurring in the square root of 1 percent of a population is able to produce a metaparadigm shift throughout the entire population. Globally, that means, given a world population of about 8 billion, a critical mass of a little more than 8,944 people living their lives in a heart-centered, enlivened, and harmonious way every day can literally change our reality. For this to happen, we need to be willing to open up our creative ways of thinking about ourselves and the world.

Creative energy is a life-giving force that unbinds our imagination, supports our capacity for brilliant innovation, and aids in the implementation of unique, new solutions. It's a kind of inherent superpower that engages aspects of us that are capable of incorporating the intelligence of body and soul as well as a spacious nonlinear mind. This energy is so powerful that tyrannical governments seek to restrain it by shutting down creative people. While these law-and-order, doctrine-following authorities are invested in oppressing anything that challenges the status quo, creative energy is ingenious. Creativity actively seeks new horizons. It cannot be bound. It is an energy that, like water, always finds a way to flow.

In these pages, I'll be sharing shamanic perspectives about what creative energy encompasses, how it works, how it is connected to your health and well-being, what interferes with creative flow, how you can enhance your native creative abilities, how to get unstuck, and how you can use the ancient methods of shamanism to transform your whole brain into a creative energy machine. The exercises throughout the book are some of the tools I have learned on my own path, which I'm certain will serve you, too.

Over the decades of dancing with my own creative energy and my experiences with shamanism, studying with Western shamanic teachers and some truly marvelous indigenous shamans from around the world, I have come to understand that the health of our body, mind, and spirit is intimately connected to the flow of personal creative energy. Creative energy is an essential aspect of what makes and remakes the body, expands mental abilities, and rejuvenates the spirit.

In addition, I realized that my years of shamanic work provided me not only with the ability to mentally expand into altered states and discover practical ways to solve problems, it also heightened my creative energy immensely. This was a stunning revelation for me as, prior to my shamanic exploration, I had already been a visual artist, illustrator, art director, museum exhibits designer, mask and costume creator, and a maker in many other ways. Yet something had happened to me through my use of the shamanic technologies of journeying and ceremonies: they had expanded my creative capacity in directions I had never believed possible.

I also realized that I could completely take the leash off creative energy and give it free rein in my life. When I threw away any limiting ideas about my creativity, including how I had to define myself as a creative person, I became truly free to let my creativity flow in any direction that it wanted.

During my explorations, I learned that creative energy is so powerful that it provides more return than is expended in its use. Any time you allow your creative energy an outlet to flow, you receive a net gain of energy. Creative energy is always present, and when we give it permission, it can effortlessly flow in innumerable directions. It may sound too fantastic to believe, but the years I've spent in my studio and at the side of indigenous shamans have proven to me otherwise.

This book is meant to support your own unique and wonderful creative energy to open up and flourish. Even if you are already aware of your creative nature, I hope you'll use this book to learn more about your own creative energy and boost your abilities to the next level. No matter how creative you believe yourself to be, I've learned firsthand that creativity actually has no limiting threshold. *Ever.*

The energy of creativity can enrich all aspects of your life. It has the capacity to birth amazing new ideas and innovative possibilities that can continue expanding your experience of living in every imaginable way. Our times require everyone's creativity. Your unique and extraordinary genius needs to be awakened and encouraged as a part of transforming the minds and hearts of our collective.

It's time to embark on this adventure, together!

ONE

How Shamanic Creativity Supports Wholeness

$\int$hamanic Creativity is a pathway for opening up your life in remarkable ways. It is an energy that can support you in dealing with life's challenges with more ease and grace. It can launch you beyond your coping mechanisms into entirely new perspectives on situations, supporting growth, healing, and true transformation. Just imagine reprogramming your subconscious to know with certainty that you are more than you believe. This happens naturally as you work with the creative energy you were bestowed with at birth.

By expanding your understanding of yourself, you realize more of your inherent gifts and live more of your potential than you have currently realized. You and I are part of a creative cosmos that is endlessly modeling and reshaping matter. When we fully open ourselves to that energy and learn to work with it, we are capable of more imagination, more ingenuity, more passion and joy!

When we embark on something new and unfamiliar, we can feel nervous and even a bit anxious. This inner resistance is an energy that can shut us down and make learning difficult, so before we jump into learning more about creative energy, we'll explore how to deal with that first!

SURVIVAL MODE

When afraid, especially when fear becomes a chronic condition, people usually gravitate toward one of two strategies to feel safe. Both of these strategies are also used by animals to survive the dangers that they face.

The Bunker Method

The first survival method is one used by ground-dwelling mammals such as the woodchuck, the prairie dog, and the meerkat. It involves a contraction into the smallest space that is perceived to be farthest from the threat. In the human world, those who choose the bunker approach desire a simplistic sense of safety. Like a child hiding in a closet or dashing to hide behind her mother, bunker seekers have a subconscious desire for a space that feels small enough to be emotionally manageable, often coupled with a desire for an authority to make it all OK. They seek the comfort of absolutes, of linear paths, of dogmatic structures, or of a leader who can give them the feeling that *everything is all right*. Those that choose this method have a desire to be comforted without having to engage personal energy in a solution. As this path is passive in nature and does not demand participating in creating solutions, it can appeal more strongly to those with less education or those who have not been exposed to people different from themselves or cultures and ideologies that diverge from their own. Those who seek the shelter of the bunker can become inadvertent prey to the perceived safety and community of isolating ideologies, such as fundamentalist religions, cults, and other restrictive, carefully prescribed social orders.

The Overlook Method

On the other hand, there are animals that seek a high vantage point for survival. Like a mountain goat keeping to the promontory of a mountain or a crow on a treetop, these animals seek the bigger picture, which is also a good strategy for dealing with fear. This expansive viewpoint enables the animal to observe and manage threats.

People who use this method instinctively seek more information and a broader or different perspective to engage with their fears. They actively look for solutions to how they are feeling and are the ones who will look toward new ideas, seek out various self-help resources, use therapeutic methods, and engage in learning something new. Proponents of the overlook method have a sense that the tool for dealing with their anxiety is "out there," just over the next horizon waiting to be discovered. They know that it is up to them to put energy into the search. People who use the overlook method can usually find a path to healing. However, in some cases, this method can result in visits to many different practitioners or trying a variety of modalities in a seemingly endless search for the "right" approach that will work.

To a degree, both these methods for dealing with threats and fear are useful in temporarily quelling anxiety and also have drawbacks. I propose that there is a third way that shamanic creativity offers that can be much more effective.

THE DOORWAY TO A NEW PERSPECTIVE METHOD

A cultural trope suggests that artists must suffer for their work. Instead, I would say that artists, musicians, writers, and other creatives have developed strategies for transforming personal pain, such as anxiety, into *doorways*. The deeply creative people I know have learned through experience that their struggles can lead to new thoughts, new explorations, new bodies of work, and new inventive solutions. They have trained themselves to look at perceived internal or external threats as openings to something wonderful.

Many creative people have developed methods of self-exploration that can support them to gain a personal, higher-ground perspective. This internal process may include addressing the threat or issue at hand like a blacksmith hammering raw iron into something useful. They produce work that examines the painful stimulus from many viewpoints and, in so doing, find a way through to a new place of peace.

In others, the anxiety becomes a path inward to the deeper source of pain that requires healing or resolution. This internal digging often produces emotional gold. In either case, the trust they have developed in their creative energy provides the sustenance to keep moving through the doorway to the other side.

Portals to other ways of understanding parallel the transitional space shamans experience while traveling between the worlds.

Shamans also use doorways in their work. They use the ability to step between ordinary reality and the spirit world of pure energy to gain insight, to find hidden information, to gain knowledge, or to find the best way to solve a problem. They accomplish this by expanding their awareness so that a new perspective, approach or solution is discovered.

I believe that the confluence of flowing creative energy with the consciousness expansion developed through shamanic journeying is the most effective and productive remedy for the whole-being paralysis that overwhelms you when you are stricken with fear. These two tools move energy in a way that encompasses body, mind, and soul.

I want to share a vivid memory from my childhood to help you better understand my ideas about creativity as a living energy.

The memory begins with me standing at the top of a wooden staircase that snakes down to a sandy beach. I've paused at this vantage point to look out at the ocean. The air around me is saturated with light bouncing back and forth between the surface of the water and the atmosphere, and the salt-laden breeze is blowing my hair.

The tide is just right on this trip. Not too high so that it swallows the beach or too low, causing the waves to break on the rougher sand, filled with broken shells. This is a perfect day! I had been watching older kids body surf and had studied the moves they'd made to be lifted up and carried into shore. Through trial and error, I figure out my method. Turned on a 45-degree angle to the surf, I watch the waves and jump up with each one, practicing my timing. If you jump and lunge forward too late, you are likely to come back down into water that is over your head. If you jump too early, you could be swamped and tumbled roughly around until you are spit out onto the beach with a swimsuit full of sand.

Positioning myself in the water, I jump and try a few lunges until my timing is perfect. A wave gathers me up and carries me on my belly all the way back to the beach. The feeling of being supported by the energy of the water is amazing! I keep going back in the surf until my legs are wobbly with exhaustion.

Each time the wave carries me, the sense of the effort I expended becomes irrelevant. I am experiencing a total surrender to the energy of the sea.

Like the ocean's waves, creative energy is present all the time. Even when the ocean looks calm, the deep waves and currents are still generating movement. Creative energy is rhythmic, having its higher and lower periods that are like the ocean's tides. It can be stirred by your conscious actions in the way wind whips the ocean into great waves. And creative energy can lift you up on a joyously exhilarating ride—if you are willing to expend a little effort in understanding how it works and how to encourage it!

My desire is to blow the lid off the cultural conspiracy that sug-

Memories can be encoded with new perspectives
when viewed years later.

gests that only certain special people are creative. You are the product of many thousands of generations of remarkable people who were inspired to bring forth new, ingenious solutions that allowed them to survive and thrive. This energy is part of *every* human being's genetic legacy. (And yes, I mean *you,* too!) I want you to know the certainty of it, be able to enhance it, and embolden its capacity to transform how you live your life. Creative energy has life-giving benefits and stimulates the soul.

Furthermore, *there is no limit to how creative you can become.* Even as a highly creative thinker, I have unlocked a great deal more creative potential through practicing the techniques in these pages. Through experience, I now believe that it's possible to continue enhancing your creativity for as long as you live.

YOUR CREATIVITY MAKES YOU *YOU!*

Could you imagine a world that never changed, a nature that didn't continually experiment with life-forms for new circumstances or different habitats, a cosmos without new stars being born? I certainly can't.

Creative energy is intrinsic. It flows throughout everything and exists everywhere. It's also a constant. If it weren't for creative energy, our world—indeed the cosmos itself—would become static and devoid of life. In whatever way you may label the universal consciousness of which we are a part and that moves through us and also continually remakes us, I think you'd agree that it is nothing if not creative!

In addition, since everything and every being is part of that ever-creative cosmos, it must mean you and I were meant to express that energy. After all, there are tangible examples of creative energy working its regenerative magic in your physical body. Your cells are refreshed with new ones on a regular basis. Your tissues are capable of repairing torn flesh, and your fingernails and hair grow continually. This is your body at work, creating new cells. It doesn't require much searching to realize that you and I are fully submerged in creative energy all the time.

Your creative energy matters because you are a cell in the greater organism of Earth. Just as every cell in a body needs to be online for your body to function well, you, as a cell of Earth's body, need to be on full power, too. The ideas, thoughts, and feelings within you might well be what is most needed now. We can't know what power our creativity may have. When we give creative energy our full permission, we become conduits for something much larger than we are.

I believe that our collective creativity is essential for creating new realities. Those of us who choose to use our creativity to the fullest, directing it for life-sustaining purposes, are the ones who will support our culture to throw off outdated philosophies that limit our powers for a new kind of greatness. *By unleashing our most creative selves, we become the potential for nothing less than a future that is visionary, healing, sustaining, and regenerative for all beings.*

Oh, and by the way, if you think what you just read was nonsense, Fortune 500 companies would beg to differ. The largest and most successful companies in the world are all actively promoting creativity in their employees. They wouldn't use resources for this purpose if creativity wasn't something that could make a company grow or become more profitable. *In truth, creative energy is more precious than gold.* The flow of creative energy is a life-giving force that, when unleashed, is also self-sustaining. When it is encouraged and we learn to work with it and step out of its way, creative energy delivers more to us than we put in. In that way, it is like nothing else I know.

When creative energy is flowing, it:

- Allows you to see a problem in ways that are different from other people's views
- Gives you the energy to take risks (however small or large) that other people are afraid to take
- Imparts courage to stand up for your fresh perspectives
- Encourages the ability to overcome obstacles and directly challenge the way it is and manifest what can be

To be able to work with your creativity, it is also useful to develop a reliable method for rebalancing yourself. This is important as exercising the creative, nonlinear mind can sometimes disturb the part of us that likes a tidy, predictable world. You see, the linear, ordinary thinking that you use in everyday life has been your gatekeeper. It has functioned to store all of your previous experiences and cautiously review all new input. Since opening up your creative energy is a series of out-of-the-box experiences, the linear mind may try to shut it down because it is nearly always hesitant to make changes that disrupt its carefully controlled sense of order. Your linear mind may try interrupting you when you are in creative thought with mundane mental pop-ups, reminding you to put mayonnaise on the shopping list or to pick up the dry cleaning. It might also become like the incessant crawl at the bottom of the news channel screen, reminding you of all the awful reasons this "creative nonsense" is to be avoided. This kind of mental sabotage is common, and so it's best to plan for it and be ready should it happen to rear its ugly head.

Whenever we learn new things, there is a period of adjustment in our subconscious mind. As we take the new information in, it may chafe against a previous notion or long-held perception about ourselves or our world. In the way that growing taller may have caused you to feel odd or be physically clumsy when you were a tween, change can be unsettling and even upsetting. It warrants slowing down a bit and being more conscious of your thoughts and actions. After all, a true transformation includes *all* of your being! You are in the process of becoming a version of yourself that is more extraordinary and beautifully brilliant.

If at any point in this book you feel uncomfortable in any way, or your linear mind starts kicking up a fuss, use the meditation below. I also suggest that you make it a part of your daily regimen. Learning to feel connected with your most expansive self while feeling your intrinsic connectedness to nature is healing, balancing, and nurturing. It will also help you to regain clarity and centeredness in any situation.

We are made from the elements of Earth and are a part of her body
and dependent on her health for our own.

(Photo by NASA)

Read the exercise through once or twice before you begin listening
to the "Tapping into the Creative Energy in and around You" meditation mp3 audio file that is available at **audio.innertraditions.com
/shacre.**

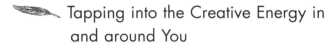 Tapping into the Creative Energy in
and around You

1. Begin by finding a quiet space where you will not be disturbed. Sit
   down in a comfortable chair that allows your back to be straight with
   your feet on the floor.

2. With your hands folded gently in your lap, close your eyes and take a few moments to breathe. Allow your breaths to be both quiet and full, somewhat like the breaths of the deep sleep state.

3. As you begin to more fully relax, notice that your breath originates in the center of your chest. Imagine a light there that grows brighter with every breath that you take.

4. As this light grows brighter, imagine it expanding to fill your entire body—growing ever brighter. Your radiant body is an expression of our cosmos of creative energy. The powerful creative force of exploding novae seeded the cosmos with all of the elements to make you and the body of our beautiful planet. All of the iron, calcium, oxygen, and other elements are gifts from the stars. This gift is what you inhabit while you are embodied. You are a divinely radiant, creative being wrapped in star stuff!

5. Allow your radiant energy to expand so that your physical body is enfolded in light. Your spirit—your light—completely surrounds your body. This is your true state of being. Your entire being is full, rich, radiant, beautiful, and alive with creative energy!

6. While continuing to breathe, notice how your creative radiance is connected to the creative radiance of the Earth. Your body moves within the atmosphere of our planet. You live by swimming through her air with your feet touching her body. Your body is held by your light and is always cradled by the Earth. Her creativity is also yours.

7. Allow yourself to reach out even farther and feel how the sun's creative, life-sustaining warmth embraces the Earth as she embraces you. Allow all your senses to be fully enlivened by this nurturance. You are a magnificently embodied aspect of the creative energy that flows throughout All That Is. You were created to be a creator in concert with Mother Earth.

8. Breathe in the depth of these creative connections between you, the cosmos, and our beautiful world and allow it to bring you to a peaceful and fully enlivened state of being. Allow yourself to feel completely and deeply peaceful in this awareness.

9. When you feel full of this experience, clasp your folded hands tightly together. As you are doing this, recall the sensations of being fully enlivened and nurtured by the creative energy that flows throughout the cosmos. Whenever you wish, you will be able to attain this feeling again by repeating this symbolic gesture with your hands.

10. Now, gently release your hands and allow yourself to slowly return your attention to the room in which you are sitting. Take a full, deep, sighing breath, and gently open your eyes.

Once you've read the meditation, find a comfortable position, and listen to the guided version through headphones. When you feel ready, you may wish to make notes about what you experienced while doing this meditation. Take time to record all that you felt, saw, and heard.

If you experienced difficulty visualizing or feeling the light at your heart center, don't worry. Sometimes it can take some time to move the consciousness down into the body and into the heart. This is especially true when we are used to being in our heads or being out of our body as a protection. Those wonderfully ingenious strategies, which may have helped us survive when we were younger, can interfere with our being able to thrive as an adult. However, with practice, you will be able to move through to a heart-centered experience.

If, on the other hand, you feel foggy, confused, or light-headed after this meditation, it means you need to practice grounding yourself. Some easy ways include:

- Eating a light snack
- Spending time outdoors, especially in a natural setting—in the woods or by the ocean or a river
- Doing something with your hands—making something, touching stones, playing in water or digging in dirt
- Sitting on the ground with your back up against a tree
- Breathing with a focus on the soles of your feet, feel them touching the inside of your shoes or the ground

- Imagining roots coming from the bottom of your feet into the ground to firmly tie you to the core of Earth
- Listening to whatever music makes you want to dance and then getting up and *dancing!*

Above all, please be gentle with yourself, especially if you feel that your experience with the meditation, or any other lesson in this book, feels difficult. You are in the process of transforming old, outmoded ideas about creativity and yourself. This procedure is something that is best done with a loving patience and a gentle persistence. Over time, a kind of softening begins to occur that gradually allows your new way of being to ease into existence.

Process Questions

- ➻ Articulate in your journal, as best you can, the bodily, emotional and spiritual sensations of being an embodied aspect of the creative energy that flows throughout All That Is.
- ➻ How do your feelings now differ from your feelings before you practiced this meditation?
- ➻ Think about how this practice could benefit your daily life. Record your impressions.

Choose a time of day to practice this meditation. Practice with the audio file once a day for at least two weeks. As you do this daily, you will be able to attain this state of being more easily. As with all things worth doing, the time you spend on this and the other exercises in this book will serve you well.

WHAT IS CREATIVITY?

As you may have already guessed, the creative label was assigned to me very early on in my life. I was given that designation because I was able to draw. What that actually means is that I had learned how to take visual input and render a reasonable version of it in two dimensions. However, a lot of that ability was gained through honing my visual perception, by practicing really seeing what was in front of my eyes and then applying untold hours of practice. Those things are part of a learned skill set, not creative energy. Yet that skill endowed me with "specialness" that the other skilled people didn't receive. No matter how much I told others that it was my practicing drawing that made the results look right, they kept praising my talent as if it were something you had to have been blessed with at birth. They usually followed up with some self-deprecating line like, "I can't draw a straight line without a ruler!" News flash: neither can I.

In my eyes, it was oddly unfair that the people who expressed their creative energy by fabricating a hot rod, producing a garment without a pattern, transforming a found object into a lamp, or developing a new recipe were considered handy or resourceful but not readily accepted at the "creative people table" in the same way artists and writers were. This inequity was set in the wide-held belief that a person's creative ability was defined by a narrow set of culturally prescribed ideals. Of course, nothing could be further from the truth. All of society's acclaimed great works of art, music, and literature are really only the footprints left behind by the creative energy of someone who had sharply honed a specific set of skills. Cultural values were then placed on these by-products based on the subjective opinions of individuals that have been awarded expert status, some of whom benefit directly in the marketing of creativity.

If we stop accepting that only poems, songs, paintings, or sculptures are proof of creativity, we can then see that people who shape steel into a fender, wool into a garment, and broken china into a mosaic or who manifest ideas they conceived in their heads and hearts are all conduits and participants in creative energy's flow.

Author, artist, and workshop facilitator Lucy Pearce suggests that creativity is a "revolutionary act" in that it is an imaginative way of approaching life and its challenges.[1] I also believe that creativity is natu-

Just as fingerprints are never mistaken for the person who left them, works of creativity must not be equated with the energy of creativity.

ral force with its own pulse, rhythm, and flow. It produces more energy than is expended in its use and is capable of enlivening all aspects of life. Not only that, creative energy is installed as standard equipment in every model, shape, and size of human being.

Learning to flow with creative energy is a dynamic process that uses various brain states. This process may be triggered when we perceive a problem has arisen. The conundrum we face might be practical, esoteric, or a blend of the two that requires a solution. The brain analyzes the situation and then begins shuffling data and thoughts around. If we give our brain free rein—which is a learnable skill—our ordinary, analytical brain state begins to step down from its place of dominance. At this point, the more spatial, nonlinear, imaginative, emotional, and intuitive brain activity begins to whir so that images and seemingly random or especially unique ideas begin to arise. Through this process, cognitive leaps are often made. Our brain then processes all this data to synthesize new connections. If we have learned to use our brain's full range of awareness, we can allow our spacious, nonlinear mind to season the process with intuitive leaps and a liberal dose of imagination, and soon we have a solution to implement.

That may sound complicated, but in truth you were born with the ability to do all of it.

Creative energy is one of the essential elements we have as human beings. It has been described as a divergent way of thinking that is nonlinear and that can generate multiple solutions to open-ended, unscripted problems. It's what facilitates the flow of imagination, innovation, and invention, which can continually transform our reality.

Creative energy allows us to:

- Visualize new possibilities
- Innovate new solutions
- Invent new things
- Solve complex problems

In other words, what we understand as creativity is actually the flow state of creative energy.

Dr. Amit Goswami refers to four kinds of creative energy flow. The one he labels *fundamental* is a kind that brings forth ideas that are wholly original in that it not only offers a new solution but it also transforms the context in which the question existed. Those who first pioneered new ideas about physics could be put into that category as their solutions to cosmic questions arose not just as unique ideas in and of themselves, but they also simultaneously challenged and rose beyond the established Newtonian ideas in physics.

Situational creative energy flow functions within a specific context but also finds new ways to work using other established contexts. The smartphone is an example of a situational creation: it expands wireless communication, but it also performs a variety of other functions that a slew of separate devices once provided. This handheld device, with seemingly endless functionality, has eliminated the need for a watch, a camera, a notebook, a music player, and a GPS, and it also includes a computer with access to the internet.

Goswami also suggests that there is both *inner* and *outer* creative flow. Outer creativity affects the world around us by generating objective products and includes both fundamental and situational creativity. Whereas inner creativity is an internal paradigm shift occurring within a person's consciousness that allows a new context of experiencing and living life that may or may not lead to an outer expression of creativity.

THE PATHWAYS AND PROCESSES OF CREATIVE ENERGY

Simply put, that which we call creativity is the action of bringing a unique but intangible "something" (a thought, idea, or feeling) into existence. This manifested idea *may* produce some form of object or an experience but does not depend on it, nor does such an object define it. *It is the energy that matters!* However nonlinearly it travels, creative energy is understood to have a path. Nearly a hundred years ago, Graham Wallas suggested that creative energy in action has four phases: *preparation, incubation, sudden insight,* and *manifestation.*[2]

Preparation is the time when a glimmer of an idea or concept is just beginning to brew in your mind. During this phase, you might do a lot of research, thinking, and note taking. This is a time of intense effort, during which you saturate yourself with everything about the question or problem at hand.

The *incubation* period is a time when the imagination must be given the full freedom to play, experiment, and develop the idea while you actually apply less effort. This is when the subconscious can take over the task of playing with the idea while you are engaged in activities like taking a walk, performing mundane tasks, or even sleeping. During this time, conscious activity is suspended while the subconscious mind sifts through all the data you have given it and mixes it with the unique insights only its nonlinear nature can provide.

In the *sudden insight* period, the subconscious delivers the product of its illuminative efforts to the conscious mind. This is the time you capture the insights in notes and sketches so that they can be refined during the next phase of *manifestation.* This stage is the period when the conscious mind takes all the input it has received and churns, examines, and evaluates to come up with a final solution for the circumstance.

This way of looking at the aspects of the creative process may seem to imply that the process is linear in nature, but this is certainly not true! Creative energy often flows in both a circular and a branching fashion; processing may happen on several strands simultaneously. Creative energy bushwhacks new paths of thought—climbing over previous assumptions and turning old ideas over to see if new ones lie below—and stumbles into incredible vistas along the way, which inspire further new pathways. A creative cycle may go from preparation to sudden insights, to incubation, back to preparing again, and so forth with no idea of following a prescribed pathway other than that of its own design. It is a flow of thinking and applying effort and then allowing imagination and the subconscious to percolate before consciously thinking and applying effort again. This cycle may happen more than once in the development of a solution.

In its workings, creative energy may take something used for one purpose and repurpose it for an entirely new use. This is what evolutionary biologists refer to as *exaptation,* a word coined by evolutionary biologists Elisabeth Vrba and Stephen Jay Gould. Exaptation refers to a trait that was originally created through natural selection for one purpose but is then co-opted for a new function.

Examples of exaptation in the natural world include feathers, which originally evolved in dinosaurs for insulation or mating displays but later became useful for flight; the skull sutures found in all vertebrates, which allowed for brain growth but were co-opted for another purpose in mammals to allow the skull of a fetus to compress as it passes through the birth canal; and genetic material left behind by viruses, which plays an important role in mammalian pregnancy. Furthermore, it is suggested that every evolutionary adaptation was accompanied by multiple potential exaptation processes. In essence, part of nature's tool kit involves a "using what's readily at hand" method for solving problems. Through experimentation, exaptation successfully adapts something for other than its original purpose.[3] Your creative energy works the same way. The act of taking some odd thing you found at the flea

Nature transforming the purpose of a feather is one tiny example of her endless creativity.

market and turning it into a beautiful piece of unique furniture and, indeed, the whole genre of creative upcycling are examples of exaptation in action.

Along with exaptation, creative energy has other components that are part of the nonlinear progression of ideas. Wallas's sudden insight aspect of the creative process can certainly be a flash of intellectual insight, but it can just as easily be an instinctual gut feeling that provides a spark of an idea. These are usually a result of the subconscious mind at work—that aspect of you, lying just under your conscious awareness, that is always listening to and processing the world around you. Sparks from the subconscious may come as a feeling, an image, or a precious scrap of a day or night dream and require careful handling. They are meant to be preserved as is, without any judgment or critical response. From that point of being preserved, they then can be explored and nurtured to grow.

A creative insight may also arrive by mental "snail mail" in what Stephen Johnson in his book *Where Good Ideas Come From: The*

Natural History of Innovation refers to as the intangible "slow hunch." This is a vague notion, an intuition that there is a new idea or a way to solve a problem that itself isn't yet clear. These can steep like tea inside you for years. They wait until just the right connections evolve to bring the full idea to awareness. These hunches are also meant to be preserved in their raw state and allowed to grow inside the nonlinear mind.

The creative process also uses serendipitous dream imagery, unexpected experiences, and exchanges of ideas to bring forth those insights that lead to solutions. A classic example of this is how Friedrich August Kekulé, a German chemist, cracked the problem of understanding how the atoms of the benzene molecule were arranged. Kekulé had theorized several models for the molecule, but none of them was correct. In a dream state, Kekulé saw atoms dancing in a circle. Later in the dream, he saw a vision of the ouroboros, the snake biting its tail. In the dream state, Kekulé's nonlinear mind solved the problem that his linear mind couldn't achieve. The circular snake image stayed with him, and the following day he tested a ring form of atomic structure that turned out to be the exact solution to the problem.

Dreaming of the ouroboros inspired Kekulé to make an imaginative leap.

The creative mind at work is also capable of consciously inducing a serendipitous circumstance. In other words, using the tools of the conscious mind to prepare fertile ground for the subconscious to produce the insightful coup de grâce. This requires the cognitive ability to imagine two opposites or contradictory ideas, concepts, or images existing simultaneously. This is referred to as *Janusian thinking,* a term that references Janus, the Roman god with two faces, one looking forward and one looking backward. Although seemingly illogical and self-contradictory, constructing these conceptualizations in your mind can stimulate new and often startling ideas to emerge from your deeper consciousness. A primary feature of this process is simultaneously holding multiple opposites or antitheses in your mind. These contradictory factors could be held on a mental pinboard or captured in a notebook. If we take this a step further and allow the antithetical elements to occupy the exact same space, this is referred to as *homospatial thinking.* In this case, the two divergent concepts, ideas, or images can merge into a hybridized new idea, like taking an image of a man and an image of a horse and overlapping them, thereby producing an entirely new being, the centaur.

In the pages in this book, you'll be engaging with these concepts and methods to find ways to encourage your own creative energy to flow. For now, you will need a way to capture ideas, images, and words that are intrinsic to your own creative flow. Like so many things in life, nurturing your creative energy requires having the right tools for the job!

YOUR IDEA RECEPTACLE

Just as every wizard needs a wand, you need to *keep a notebook with you at all times.* I'm not kidding. No matter what other methods I suggest in these pages, that is a creative cardinal rule I find essential. You never know when an idea will strike. In fact, great ideas often arise when you are busily engaged with something else. I have had ideas emerge while driving, washing dishes, in an airplane, while sitting in a meeting on a completely different subject, and even in intimate moments. With my notebook nearby, I can capture an idea as soon as it is safe and appropriate for me to do so.

You may choose any shape or size notebook just as long as you can easily tote it around with you *everywhere*. You may even use a small sketchbook. I prefer a 5.5-inch by 8.5-inch size sketchbook with an elastic band that keeps it closed. The band also keeps scraps of paper I may grab to catch an idea in any odd place when I can't pull out the book.* I'm one who loves a completely blank page and abhors ruled paper for recording ideas. More often than not, I may doodle an image as well as write, and ruled lines just cramp my style. Needless to say, you'll need to carry a pencil or pen as well. By the way, in case you are thinking about just using the note feature on your smart phone, it isn't a substitute for writing with an implement on a page.

Writing in longhand has many benefits for the creative mind. First, it is inherently *slow,* which gives ideas a chance to fully emerge and to be felt and for thoughts to more completely run their course. In addition, writing in longhand fires up more of your brain! Writing with a handheld implement such as a pencil or pen helps to exercise your sensory pathways and also raises the level of the creative thoughts being written. Longhand writing stimulates better focus. Because you cannot pull up a Google window or check your social media account on a paper sketchbook or notebook, you have less opportunity to distract yourself. A notebook also doesn't tether you to a desk or an electrical outlet: you can write whenever and wherever inspiration strikes, unchaining your ability to set down your ideas. Writing in this way also takes more of the inner critic off-line as it is much harder to fiddle a sentence to death in a notebook. You are much more able to capture an idea and even a first draft of something in longhand than on a computer that keeps calling attention to your spelling, punctuation, and sentence structure with those annoying blue or red underlines.

---

*On long car rides, my partner copilot often has to write down spontaneous ideas that come to me while driving. Those scraps of paper get tucked into my sketchbook at the next rest stop.

Your idea receptacle can become a powerful tool for nurturing
and expanding your inherent creative energy.

Longhand writing also improves your memory of what you've written. By using longhand, you have engaged more of the native intelligence of your mind, but you've also engaged your body, senses, and
spirit in the process. Last, writing longhand also improves memory,
not just of what you've written but overall as you exercise several of the
brain's pathways simultaneously. Doctors who study brain function suggest that writing in this way is a great cognitive exercise that can help
you to preserve your mind's sharpness and help you to learn new skills.[4]

Haven't yet convinced you of the benefits of writing longhand?
Well, how about the idea that you'd be in awfully good company!
Well-respected and prolific authors such as Joyce Carol Oates,

Neil Gaiman, Amy Tan, Stephen King, Jhumpa Lahiri, James Patterson, and George R. R. Martin all use longhand to write their first drafts.

In addition, you are free to make diagrams, doodle, draw arrows, or circle important bits of your thinking process in a notebook without switching into another mode. You even have a basic edit tool on the back end of your pencil! As I stated earlier, I find that I am just as likely to draw, diagram, and use other visual shortcuts when using pencil or pen on a sheet of paper. Perhaps it is because I was originally trained as a visual artist that I use images as a kind of shorthand. For me, they can capture the thread of an idea faster than words can and can even capture things I wouldn't be able to hold in words. For instance, I even captured, pre-smartphone, the basic melody of an indigenous shaman's song without using traditional musical notation. I did this by using a pattern of symbols with long and short strokes and spaces. Even though the method was crude, because I had engaged my entire being in finding a way to capture the song on the page, I was able to play it on a keyboard when I got home. Since I had also written the words phonetically, I was able to catch the complete, embodied experience of the song. This provided something that an audio recording would not have done with the same degree of richness.

The ideas you write and diagram on a paper page stay with you, *and* the method will work in all kinds of situations. A notebook will never disappoint you in a power outage, give you away in a darkened room or movie theater, or distract you with texts, alerts, or a phone call. It will also make you appear really engaged in your thoughts, so strangers will be less likely to chat you up during times that you want to just sit and think. In addition, the notebook is a kind of sacred sanctuary. It has the intimacy of a diary, a quality of character that a facile device fails to hold.

Best of all, since ideas written into your sketch/notebook in longhand become strongly installed into your brain, your subconscious mind will play with them when you are busy doing something else.

DEDICATING YOUR IDEA RECEPTACLE

Whenever you feel ready, pick up your new sketch/notebook and give it
a name. Yes, you read that correctly. Instead of the book being a "what"
you are going to change it into a "who."

This sketch/notebook is about to become your creative co-
conspirator. Be playful but also respectful of the book's role in your
process as you think about a name.

The name of your book could be something like Tardis to represent
that it—like Dr. Who's transport of the same name—holds more inside
than is apparent on the outside. You may want to choose a name that
relates to fertility, flow, rivers, or creation. In this case you might choose
Mbaba Mwana Waresa, a Zulu goddess of fertility, rain, and rainbows,
or the ancient Egyptian Tefnut. A name associated with creating or
encouraging life might also be a good choice for your sketch/notebook.
Thesan was an Etruscan goddess of the dawn and the generation of new
life. Perhaps you think of the book as doorway; in that case you could
call your sketch/notebook Portunus, after the ancient Roman god of
keys and portals. If you do think of your creative receptacle book as
doorway, you may want to choose a different language's word for door.
Tür is the word for door in German, *dør* is the Norwegian and Danish
version, while *mlango* is the word in Swahili. Of course, you could also
use the word for book in another language. In Irish Gaelic it's *leabhar,*
in Lakota it's *wowapi,* while Estonian gives us *raamat.*

Whatever name you choose, it must hold meaning for you. Let
yourself be with the book, and let the feeling guide you to the right
name. Once you've chosen a name that feels right for your creative companion, perform this brief ceremony to dedicate it.

A ceremony? Yes, fresh, meaningful ceremonies have tremendous
power. They are a vital aspect of how shamans work to create harmony
and healing. Not only are ceremonies conscious actions, they also tele-
graph to the subconscious that something you are doing or thinking is
important. When, for instance, you take the time to consciously name

the notebook and dedicate it, you are telling your subconscious mind that this is a partner in your creative life, that it is important, and that anything you put in it is special. You aren't just using words but taking an action that requires some preparation, so the communication is being given to the subconscious through several channels. This is important, as the subconscious mind controls the meaning, shape, and texture of your existence.

You see, your subconscious mind is the aspect of you that has taken *everything* in, from the moment of your birth until the moment you are reading these words. It holds emotional as well as cognitive programming that was installed in your very early childhood. As a result, it has formulated perceptions and misperceptions about you and the world at large that impact everything in your life. The programming you received may have been accidental on the part of your parents or, in some cases, intentionally installed. It is where your inner sense about your inherent worth, value, and potential are held. Often, these are limiting beliefs that continue to influence how you perceive yourself and your world today. Reprogramming your subconscious mind with positive messages involves using your conscious mind, your feelings, and your physical actions to provide antidotes to the old messages. When reprogrammed, the subconscious mind can support you to manifest a more happy and successful life. Throughout this book, I'll be supporting you to reprogram your subconscious in many different ways, but for now, you will be focusing on the ceremony.

Since the subconscious mind has immense influence over how you feel and act in your life, giving it the message that you are a creative being with a specially designated tool that will assist you in bringing your creativity into the world can be a real game changer. Through this ceremony, you will begin transforming how you experience your relationship to your ideas and to the act of recording them. It is the beginning of your creative transformation.

⟿ Notebook-Naming Ceremony

To perform this ceremony of dedication, you'll need:

- Your sketch/notebook
- Your writing implement(s)
- A small bowl of water
- A feather
- A stick of incense with a scent that you find delightful with a safe container and matches
- A few small images from magazines, printed from your phone, or printed out from the internet that illustrate the feeling that the name elicits (you could use river images for flow, an ornate portal for door, etc.)
- Scissors
- A glue stick

Performing the Ceremony

1. Before you begin, set out your materials and open your book to the inner cover. Next, light your incense.
2. Using the feather, direct the smoke over your new sketch/notebook. Hold the intention that you are cleansing the book with the incense smoke from its long travels to you. While doing so, also honor the many hands that were involved in the making and finally handing of your book to you.
3. Do the same cleansing for your writing and drawing implements.
4. Next, dip the tips of the fingers you use to hold a pen or pencil into the water, and allow most of the water to drip off. Place those dampened fingertips on the very first page to "imprint" your mark on it.
5. Now, take the time to cut out the images so that they are just how you want to present them, and use the glue stick to paste them to the inner cover of your book. Leave some room for your book's name.
6. When everything is pasted, write your book's new name in the space you allotted. Say it aloud when you are through, and thank it for becoming your creative partner.

7. Finally, on the first page where you left your imprint, write your own name.

8. After you are through, sit a few moments and allow what you have done to sink in. If words or images come to you about the feeling you are developing for the book or how you experienced the ceremony, put them onto the pages of your new idea receptacle.

Whether you are recording new ideas, reflecting on a moment, capturing a line of poetry, or simply being with your soul self for a while, your idea receptacle can become your go-to place for encouraging your creative mind.

Process Questions

- ➴ Articulate, as best as you can, in your journal the bodily, emotional, and spiritual sensations of naming your sketch/notebook.
- ➴ How do your feelings about the book differ from your feelings before you did the naming ceremony?
- ➴ Record your impressions about this exercise so you can go over them again at a later time.

Remember, as you record in your book, no editing, correcting your spelling, or attending to grammar. If leaving anything in that state gives your "inner compulsive" the heebie-jeebies, remember you can always edit *after* your ideas, thoughts, and feelings are captured on the page.

TWO

Feelings: The Dance of Dissonance and Harmony

Our feelings may be the most underestimated part of our being. For years, we were schooled to believe that the thinking mind-brain was paramount. The body's intelligence was next in the hierarchy, and trailing a weak third were our heart-centered feelings. In fact, chances are you still hold some of those beliefs in your subconscious, as the programming that produced them started in earnest when you were preverbal. You may have been told to stop crying or that you were too sensitive or too emotional for a particular pursuit in life. As a result, you may have learned that feelings are a weakness that holds you back, so they are important to suppress. On the other hand, you may have just as likely reacted to these restrictions and become an angry or bitter person to survive. This can be calamitous, as suppression of feelings or holding onto anger in an attempt to feel "strong" can result in a host of acute and chronic physical illnesses, addictions, and mental illnesses, including depression or anxiety. These scenarios are especially tragic as we now know that feelings are a critical aspect of our ability to be a conscious creator.

Feelings are continually radiating from our bodies. Certain feelings are vital keys that contribute to our physical and mental health, to working toward our goals, to entering and maintaining relationships, and to every aspect of life. Other feelings can impede our health, productivity, and relationships. The good news is that it is possible to learn how to work with our feelings to positively transform our creativity and so contribute to experiencing a good life.

In the English language, we often use the words *emotion* and *feeling* interchangeably. I think it is important to begin thinking about them differently. Think of emotions as immediate responses to information we receive from the physical world as we move through our day. These initial reactions and responses are simple in nature. Environmental inputs stimulate the brain and nervous system to respond with emotions of mad, sad, glad, or scared.

On the other hand, feelings are what happen when our minds respond to the input we have received through our emotional pathways. Our minds, seeking to find order in the chaos of emotional input, try to interpret what is happening. It does that by comparing what is happening now to our previous experiences. In other words, our previous life experiences generate a kind of perceptual lens through which we view what happens, *now*. This blend of emotional input viewed through our perceptual lens creates an output of feelings. These feelings cascade energetic and biochemical messages throughout and beyond the body and, like consciousness as a whole, are nonlocal in nature.

You are influencing and being influenced by feelings every moment of every day. These feeling energies are not just your own. You and I are being bathed in other people's feeling energies. All. The. Time. This influences your personal creativity as well as what our collective manifests. However, you can learn how to refine your own feelings so that they support your well-being and creativity.

Feelings have a profound impact on your body's ability to function and your ability to think clearly. On a molecular level, they influence the epigenetic field, the way your genes express themselves. They can cause the DNA molecule to wind more tightly into what I call a "DNA cramp." This influences how your DNA replicates itself and how it creates proteins and enzymes that regulate a wide variety of basic cell functions and repair. On a gross physical level, feelings can either enhance or disrupt your body's ability to function.

Fear is the most disruptive emotional state. When you are afraid, your sympathetic nervous system kicks into gear, suggesting three possible responses to survive the danger: fight, flight, or freeze. Fight can manifest as anger, rage, judging or projecting blame on another, and dismissing the source. Flight might manifest as wanting to physically run away, turning to distractions, procrastinating to avoid the stimulus, or using substances (alcohol, narcotics, food) to the extent that you slide into numbness. Freezing involves becoming physically or mentally immobile, dissociating from the situation mentally, and going into shutdown mode.

Being stressed is actually a fear state. When stressed, your body produces different hormones from those during periods of inner harmony. Biochemicals, such as adrenaline and cortisol, flood your body, giving it the biochemical instructions to fight, flee, or freeze. This results in higher blood pressure and higher respiration rates, which can become persistent and life threatening. At the same time, fear suppresses other hormones, such as DHEA (dehydroepiandrosterone). This hormone contributes to slower aging, good cognitive function, and feelings of well-being. Furthermore, *just ten minutes of feeling fear can depress your immune response for six hours.*[1] When you are continually bathed in these feeling states, either from inside yourself or as a result of the feeling states of others, your body is impacted to the point where you can become not just sick but chronically ill.

The hormone changes that occur in a fear state increase access to the lower brain that reacts instead of responding to a situation. While that makes sense if you are being chased by a tiger or living in a war zone, it definitely isn't helpful in your ordinary life. Critically, these fear-induced physical changes also biochemically deny access to the upper, reasoning functions of your brain. As anyone who has drawn a blank while trying to answer a simple question in a stressful situation can attest, a DNA cramp limits one's memory and the ability to respond effectively. No one is at his or her best or fullest capacity when feeling angry or afraid.

When you learn how to work with your feeling states, you can influence the performance of your body, enhance your immune response, improve your ability to think clearly, and cushion yourself from the disruptive influence of others' dysregulated feeling states. To protect and even enhance your health, as well as put yourself in the optimum state for creativity, you need to learn how to work masterfully with your "inner technology."

The first step is recognizing that your feelings are sources of information that can be very useful to you. When you have a feeling, you are responding to a stimulus, and that response is usually shaded and sometimes wholly generated by a perception you hold in your subconscious. These perceptions may be the result of careful programming by your family of origin, schooling, or culture. For instance, they might be messages about how your gender, color, size, or other inherent characteristics limit who you are capable of being.

These perceptions can also be a result of the conclusions you made about yourself and the world around you before the age of seven. Developmentally, a child younger than seven cannot separate what is happening around her or him from what is inside. The inability to understand that what is happening outside you is beyond your sphere of influence could have caused a lot of confusion. For instance, if your parents fought constantly, you may have concluded that you caused them to fight, or that you are bad, or that they don't love you, or that you aren't good enough to stop the situation, or that the world is an inherently unsafe place—or some other negative perception about you or the world at large. Some decisions go further back to when you were a tiny, preverbal infant. In the absence of having more conscious adults to help you to repair your understanding about what was happening around you, these erroneous conclusions can become part of the perceptual lens from which you view everything.*

This lens then prescribes your response to all future situations when fear is triggered. So, if at thirty-five years old your boss harshly criticizes

---

*Repair by parents of a child's erroneous conclusions is far more likely to occur today due to better understanding about the nature of child development and the rise of disciplines such as pre- and perinatal psychology.

you, you may have feelings that you should quit because "he's probably right," or "I'm not good enough," or "I've failed again"—or some other response that was actually created in childhood. By observing how you respond to situations, you can begin to get a handle on what outmoded software in the subconscious needs updating.

While the feeling input you and I receive is often not under our influence, changing the perceptions that influence our feeling output is. Through self-observation, it's possible to alter the learned reactions that are embedded in you and thus a part of your consciousness. Through changing your perceptions and consequently changing your reactions, you will shift the vibrations you put into the world. You need feelings to inform you about what perceptions lie beneath your everyday awareness, but you also need to be able to release those feelings that disrupt your health and well-being, once you receive their messages.

PRACTICING GRATITUDE

To have your body function optimally, to have *all* of your brain online, and to begin using your creative consciousness in an intentional way, it is necessary to develop a gratitude practice. Now, you've probably heard from all the self-help gurus out there that this is a great idea, but the truth is, cultivating a state of gratitude has been a vital part of the shamanic tool kit from time immemorial. Why? Those ancient visionaries figured out that being in a state of gratitude aligns you with universal creative energies. In other words, they figured out the new physics theory about the invisible world creating physical reality many millennia ago.

Having a gratitude practice actually means *feeling* grateful as often as possible in the day. Researchers have discovered that when you feel genuine feelings of gratitude or love, you radiate an antidote to the damaging effects of fear and anger.* As stem cell biologist and bestselling author Bruce Lipton has said, "fear causes 90% of the illness on the planet. And

---

*An extensive collection of this work can be found at www.heartmath.com/research.

Making a physical offering of your gratitude outdoors each day can be a life-changing experience. Whatever safe substance you use—a few pinches of cornmeal, flowers, or a spontaneous song—concretizes your feelings into an action. In so doing, you teach your subconscious that the world is constantly showering you with blessings.

it's all generated by the perceptions of the mind. The picture you hold in your mind creates the behavior and biology you express in life."[2]

Developing a practice of gratitude can begin very simply. Take a moment each day to remember a situation when you felt grateful. Recall the feelings that you experienced at that time and let them fill you up again. Give yourself the time to feel really full. Now imagine that these feelings filling you up have nowhere else to go but to radiate out of your body. Imagine that they pulse into the environment with every one of your heartbeats and you remain full even as this vibration of gratitude is being broadcast.

I suggest that you make a gratitude list in your sketch/notebook. As you write down the situations or experiences that triggered feeling grateful, allow yourself to feel them again. This time, let yourself really revel in the feelings. This is a way to start making you more resilient to life's stressors. I use a metaphor that is firmly rooted in being a mechanic's daughter. I can't control the bumps in the road, but I can glide over them in the cushioned ride of a vintage Cadillac instead of experiencing those same bumps in the equivalent of an old Jeep. Gratitude can do just that!

RELEASING FEELINGS THAT CRAMP YOUR DNA

Life happens, and you are bound to experience feeling angry, anxious, judgmental, accusatory, and all the other faces that fear wears during your day. These feelings are all part of being human. However, you don't have to stay stuck in them or suffer the physical effects that they can cause. It is possible to learn how to get out of fear states and return to gratefulness. In this way, you can repair the effects of your DNA cramp.

Below is a step-by-step exercise that you can practice that can help you to "flip the switch" back into a healthful feeling state when it occurs. Having this in your creative toolbox will help you to become more resilient in the face of our stressful times.

Bear with me here as I explain this process. I'm going to use another car analogy.

Experiencing a DNA cramp is a lot like having your standard transmission car stuck in reverse. In such a vehicle, you can't get back into a forward gear unless you go through neutral. The exercise starts with breathing with a focus on your heart for ten to fifteen breaths or until you feel yourself beginning to relax. That state is neutral.

What follows is remembering a time that you felt grateful so that you actually reexperience the feelings. If one memory doesn't begin to elicit the feelings after a few breaths, go to another one and try again. (This is why I have developed a library of memories to support getting into gratitude more easily.) Once you are really feeling grateful, you are back in forward gear. In that state, you are repairing the damage the DNA cramp did to your immune system.

There is another really important thing to consider. Your feelings are an energetic aspect of your consciousness and are not limited by space-time. As a result, the effects of your feelings are not limited to your body alone. Your radiated feelings affect the health and well-being of every living creature around you. A study done in the 1990s by the HeartMath Institute proved that feelings produced immediate effects on identical samples of DNA from a human placenta. Indeed, the effects of both fear and gratitude on those samples were observed over a distance of half a mile (0.8 km).[3] There was no time lag, and the changes to the DNA molecules in those two research facilities, observed with identical equipment, were the same. Since feeling energies are nonlocal in nature, we do not yet understand how large their sphere of influence may be. You see, nonlocal energy itself is not measurable, only the effects are.

The point is that your feelings are contagious. When you are in a DNA cramp, the energies you emit spread out in all directions, weakening your and all other physical bodies. However, when you feel gratitude, you not only heal the effect on your DNA of your own cramp but also of other beings around you. Not only that, if others around you become agitated, afraid, or angry, you can prevent a negative effect on your body and of others nearby by going into gratitude. In essence, when you learn to switch into feeling gratitude and practice it daily, you become a form of medicine for yourself, for others, and for Earth herself.

Let that sink in.

What this means is that you can choose to create healing in the world any moment of the day. All it takes is actively reversing the damaging effects of your fear-based feelings as they occur and living more of your day in gratitude. That is an act of incredible creativity you may never have imagined. As a plus, cultivating this way of being can greatly enhance how you not only approach life's challenges but also enhance your overall well-being. This way of being has been shown to have protective effects in that it helps to bring your baseline up so that the damaging effects of your DNA cramps don't bring you

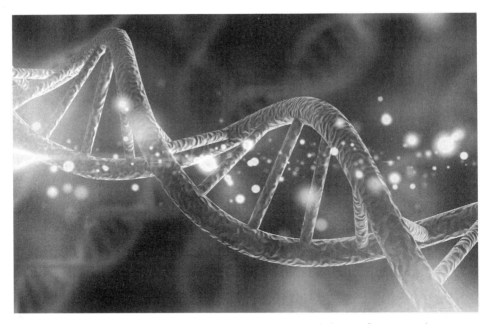

Your DNA responds to your feeling states, and the conformational
changes these feelings create can affect your health and
the health of those around you.

as far down. You become a more resilient and buoyant vessel in the
turbulent sea of life and actually help to calm the waters for all the
other boats.

Now that I've whet your appetite, what follows here are the steps
to getting back into balance after an episode of feeling angry or afraid.
It is a simple process and something you can do easily any place at
any time. I have provided an mp3 file of a guided version of the
"Repairing Your Energy after Experiencing Fear or Anger" exercise at
audio.innertraditions.com/shacre to help you more easily internalize
the method.

Read through the exercise once or twice before you begin listening
to the audio file. Make sure you have gathered a few good gratitude
memories in your sketch/notebook so you can easily recall one or more
during the exercise.

Repairing Your Energy after Experiencing Fear or Anger

The steps involved in this practice are easy to learn and simple enough to do several times a day, as they involve your internal self. No one will notice you doing this, and when you become adept at it, you can use this method to become a healing force—not only for yourself but also for those around you.

1. Wherever you are, stop for a few moments and be still.
2. In your stillness, begin breathing through your nose. As you are breathing through your nose, bring your attention to the center of your chest.
3. Imagine that you are breathing with your heart. Your breath is being drawn in by your heart as a healing balm.
4. Imagine that each breath is clearing the heart of the burden of your fear or anger. Like an ocean wave erasing marks in the sand, your breaths are smoothing . . . calming . . . clearing.
5. As you continue this way of breathing, notice your pulse slowing and your body beginning to relax. Continue breathing like this for at least ten to fifteen breaths. Take as much time as you need.
6. While continuing to breathe, begin remembering a time when you felt grateful. It can be a feeling memory from the recent or distant past. Allow yourself to fill with the feelings of that remembered moment. Remember the scene in as much detail as you are able, and let the feelings of that time fill you up again.
7. Give yourself full permission to feel the fullness of gratitude—as if what you are remembering is happening now, in this present moment.
8. Once you really feel full of gratitude, imagine those feelings radiating out from your body with each of your heartbeats. Those pulses of gratitude are bathing every person and every other living being around you in a healing, balancing energy.
9. Allow these healing feelings to radiate out in all directions. Imagine

that you are bathing all of nature with your beautiful, feeling medicine of gratitude! Expand this sphere of gratitude as far as you are able until you feel complete and balanced.

10. Slowly return your attention to where you are in physical reality. Gently return to the present moment again by smiling and taking a full, deep sighing breath.

Listen to the guided meditation mp3, and practice it at least twice daily so that you really internalize the process. This is an important part of developing emotional intelligence and is necessary for becoming a joyful, balanced, and effective creative person. Practice until you can easily shift out of negative emotions anyplace and in any situation. I cannot stress enough how critically important this ability is to your physical, mental, and ultimately creative health.

As you continue to practice daily, keep journaling what you realize about your process. This self-knowledge is important, as it is one of the keys to becoming a productive creative person.

Something else: If, in working with your feelings, you notice that you have fearful or angry feelings that appear often, you are being given vital information by your body. Those feelings are letting you know that you have a perceptual rut in your subconscious mind that is triggering that repetitive response. This is most likely a misperception about you or your world that you learned in childhood. Use your sketch/notebook to process it and see what you learn. Be gentle with yourself in your examination of those feelings, and if you get stuck, get some support. Remember, you're worth it!

Process Questions

➥ Articulate in your journal, as best as you can, the bodily, emotional, and spiritual sensations of learning how to transform the harmful effects of fear and anger.

➥ How have your ideas about feelings changed?

➥ How do you think this new awareness will change how you choose to work with your feelings?

- ✦ Will you use this method of shifting yourself when faced with another person's anger or anxiety?
- ✦ Record your impressions about this exercise so you can go over them again at a later time.

CLEARING THE FLOW OF CREATIVE ENERGY

Now that you have some ideas of what creativity is, as well as some clues about how it works, it is time to discover what hampers creative energy.

Don't Buy By-products

Chances are you (like all the rest of us) were programmed by our culture to believe that a beautiful painting, a moving piece of music, a compelling novel, or a thrilling theater piece defined real creativity. Caught in this snare of cultural programming, you may have chosen to erase yourself out of the creative picture if you produced something you liked but that was not received well by others or (worse yet) considered yourself unable to produce something you felt was "good enough." The invalid, soul-sucking equation of "great product equals creativity" has suffocated the flow of creative energy in too many people for far too long.

The tangible things that creative energy produces are not creativity; they are by-products. They are like footprints that creative energy leaves behind. Just as our focus is on the animal or person who left tracks in the woods, we have to redirect our internal gaze when we think about creativity. While these by-products are "culturally sanctioned" and usually monetized ideals of what creativity is, they are simply the evidence that creative energy has been present in abundance and that some person, with well-honed, acquired skills, rode that wave with authority and finesse.

If you're a person trying to eat in a healthier manner, you wouldn't deliberately choose to eat junk food that's laced with a bunch of unpronounceable chemical compounds. That would be contrary to your intent. Well, as an inherently creative person, you also need to make sure that you stop consuming expired, junk-food ideas about creativity. It's time to refocus on the energy of creativity. When that flow is humming, it will naturally leave a trail of fabulous ideas and products in its wake.

If you decided years ago that you're not creative and stopped expressing your creative energy, you are hereby given permission to throw off your self-devised shackles! As a human being, you were born creative. It's part of the wiring you received from your deepest ancestors. You are a product of thousands of generations of creative people. Remember it, repeat it, post it, chant it: you are creative. And get cracking!

Minding Your Minds

People who follow the structure of what has been done before rarely have fresh ideas, as they have bound themselves to the predictable, rational mind. In so doing, they have shut the door to innovation and traded it for a "safe" banality. Of course, we cannot toss the rational mind completely away. We need it to negotiate the world. The rational mind is an excellent tool for implementation. Like a well-trained team leader, it will organize and attend to details, make lists, and follow through. The trouble is that it is fairly awful at blazing new trails because it is primarily designed to follow a preset map. To explore new horizons of thought, it is necessary to become more facile with allowing your nonlinear mind to lead the expedition and then consciously choose when to use the rational, linear mind's skill set.

Being process oriented is a vital tool for unleashing your creative energy. True, you may have a specific problem to solve. However, that problem can have a myriad of solutions that your mind doesn't yet know. If you are focused on a solution, the linear mind tends to rework things it *believes* will work and eschew the gold that may be lying nearby.

The real creative treasures are found by stepping into the nonlinear mind state, and I'll guide you through exercises as we go along to support that shift.

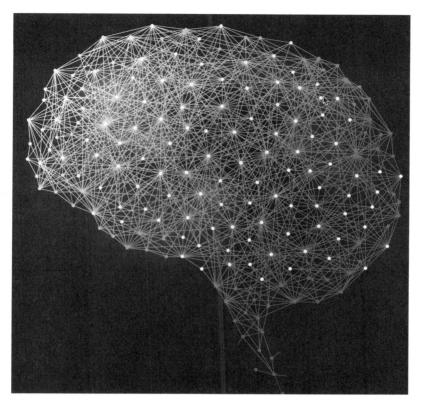

Letting your mind go off leash means giving yourself
permission to allow information or possible solutions
to arise without force.

Focusing on the Process and Letting Go of Outcome

Creative people have honed the ability to enter into a dance with their own ideas; they know how to let those ideas evolve by giving them free rein. By that I mean they choose not to clutch onto a fresh idea or project and immediately use the linear mind to set up a map or guide to achieve or manifest what they envisioned. Instead, the creative person allows the process of fruition to be organic and fluid. The original idea then has the opportunity to evolve and shift into something better, as the process of working with it unfolds.

Initially, this isn't easy as it requires both trust in self and in the force of creative energy. You learn how to trust that your "great" idea won't go away, that there may be an even better idea around the corner, and that the solution to a creative problem can have many solutions. Indeed, by trusting in the process, you may find that you were actually focused on the wrong puzzle. In other words, when you shift the focus from having a fixed goal to one of process, you open the mind to a wider landscape of thought.

As you become more adept at being process oriented, you will realize better and more amazing results. This is because the nonlinear mind has no preconceptions about the problem. It has the ability to nimbly perceive the world with fresh perspective, and *that* is a foundational root of creativity.

But What If . . . ?

Fear is the biggest creativity crusher I know. It wears a hundred masks, and any one of them can paralyze the creative process. They are also healable. Recognizing that they are residues from old experiences is a first step. A second step is realizing that every creative person I know has had to work through them. You were infected by these "computer viruses" through the enculturation you received from your family of origin, your schooling, and perhaps even your religious upbringing. The good news is that because these misperceptions are learned responses, they are within your power to change. I liken them to the country of Yugoslavia. While it was once on every map of Europe, it no longer exists. Instead, Bosnia and Herzegovina, Croatia, Macedonia, Montenegro, Serbia, Slovenia, and Kosovo have replaced it. If you are old enough (like me) to have memorized Yugoslavia as a country in Europe, you have had to replace that information with the new regions. Old, outmoded ideas are simply no longer valid.

A fear may reveal itself as a lack of trust in yourself or your talents.

In that case, you may have thoughts such as, "Who am I to write this book?" or "I have nothing to say that anyone would be interested in," or "I'll never be any good."

When the fear hasn't got you in its grip, try developing a few really good answers to those questions and write them in your sketch/notebook. Make sure to reword them in a positive way, like these:

I am the right one to [write, paint, say, compose, sing, etc.] that because no one else has my unique experience and perspective.

Of the billions of people on this planet, I know there are many people who need to experience what I [write, paint, say, compose, sing, etc.].

What I [write, paint, say, compose, sing, etc.] only gets better with each effort.

Once you have made your positive statements, make sure to say, sing, write, dance, paint, or express them *every day,* until you truly believe them. Make your expressions of these new messages bold, unapologetic, and beautiful.

Fear may also show itself as inhibitions about expressing yourself. In that case, you may have thoughts such as: "I can't paint that image. What would [insert person/people here] think?" "I can't write that story. It's too [insert reason here]." "What if people laugh at me?" These fears are based in shame. They are from an earlier experience when you were critiqued harshly, ridiculed (ah, the joys of middle school), or humiliated. In holding onto those fears, you have internalized the bullies who tried to diminish you in an effort to ensure their own sense of being powerful.

Using a little creative destruction can be very useful in releasing an internalized bully. Gather the materials, and read over the directions a few times before you perform this ceremony.

Ceremony for Slaying the Bully's Words

For this exercise, you'll need:

- Magician's flash paper, about 8 by 4 inches*
- Some felt-tip markers
- A metal baking pan or other firesafe place to burn the flash paper
- Matches or a lighter
- A celebratory snack

Performing the Ceremony

1. Set up your space where you plan to do your ceremony. Make sure your space is firesafe.

2. Clear away anything from the area that might inadvertently get burned. Also, if you have long hair, tie it back, and change if you are wearing flammable clothing.

3. Once everything is prepared, use your markers to write the bully's words on the paper. Use colors that reflect how those words may have hurt you.

4. When you have filled that paper, crumple it and set it into the pan, fireplace, or other firesafe place.

5. Light a match or strike the lighter, and in a loud voice say, "What was said to me was wrong. I do not agree with it or believe it. Those words were worthless and need to go!"; then light the edge of the crumpled flash paper. The flash paper will go up *very* fast, so make sure you choose an edge close to you so that your hand, clothing, and hair will be well out of the way.

6. Wash your hands to rid yourself of the chemicals from the paper, and then partake of your celebratory snack. Dancing, singing, and other forms of exuberance are encouraged.

---

*Flash paper is a highly flammable, tissue-like sheet of nitrocellulose impregnated with a nitrating agent. It burns quickly and completely when ignited, leaving no residue behind. Online magic shops sell flash paper in two sizes: 2 inches by 3.5 inches (5.1 cm by 8.9 cm) and 8 inches by 9 inches (20.32 cm by 22.86 cm). I recommend using half a sheet of the larger size for this ceremony.

Once you have finished celebrating, write in your sketch/notebook to capture the feelings and any thoughts that may have arose. Put the rest of your flash paper away in a safe place (I use a glass jar with a tight-fitting metal lid) for a future ceremony.

Process Questions

- ➥ As best as you can, describe in your sketch/notebook how it felt to burn the words of the bullies in your life!
- ➥ As time passes, notice what has shifted inside you as a result of this ceremony.
- ➥ How might you use this flash paper to release other outmoded ideas about yourself?
- ➥ Record your impressions so you can go over them again at a later time.

As a person raised in a society that values product and pays little attention to process, you may also have a fear about making mistakes. Believe me when I tell you, *no* brilliant creative work has ever come to fruition without being scrubbed out, painted over, erased, or edited. The fear of mistakes often expresses itself as an unrealistic and restrictive perfectionism. This fear manifests as an inner tyrant who badgers you with thoughts that you are underperforming or incapable or that your action may result in your being ridiculed. This restriction can become so powerful that it shuts off your creative flow completely.

If making mistakes is something that plagues you, it is time to make friends with the eraser. Indeed, even if you only have a mild case of this malady, I recommend that this ceremony be performed. It is fun and lighthearted and will result in a talisman that is useful beyond its original purpose!

The Holy Eraser Talisman Ceremony

For this you'll need to find a really cool eraser. These come in all kinds of shapes and sizes, from the big Pink Pearl wedged rectangle ones that have

Today, you can get erasers in an unbelievable array of shapes and sizes. Finding a fun shape will support the perception that mistakes are paths to new ideas.

been around for decades to ones shaped like everything from dinosaurs to fruit and vegetables to sushi. Choose one that you love and that you can easily carry around with your sketch/notebook.

To perform this ceremony, you'll need:

- Your special eraser
- A length of sturdy cord that, when tied into a necklace, will be long enough to pull over your head
- A strong, sharp needle to poke a large enough hole in your eraser to pull the cord through

Performing the Ceremony

1. Set up your space where you plan to do your ceremony. Make sure you have cleared away objects that might interfere or distract you.
2. Set out your materials, and thread your needle with the cord.

3. Gently twist the needle into and through the eraser as if it were a drill. Once it pokes through, twist it a bit more to gently open up the hole a little more.

4. Thread your cord through the eraser, and adjust the cord so that the eraser is centered on it. Tie a knot in your cord at a length that will allow it to go over your head easily later on.

5. Now, close your eyes while holding the threaded eraser in both of your hands. Use the "Repairing Your Energy after Experiencing Fear or Anger" exercise (page 45) you have already learned to fill with the feelings of gratitude.

6. Once you feel full of gratitude, speak aloud this magical phrase: "My mistakes are colorful stepping-stones to great ideas." Repeat this creativity incantation at least three times.

7. Place the talisman around your neck, and say the magical phrase again.

8. Open your eyes, and take a deep breath.

Make sure to say those words each time you put the talisman on. On days you can't wear it because it doesn't go with your evening gown or tux, be sure to tie it to your sketch/notebook, which you slip into your evening bag or pocket. (Remember, no exceptions. Carry your idea receptacle everywhere.)

Now, if necklaces aren't your thing, you can make earrings or pocket pieces out of your erasers, but whatever form they might take, make sure you let them become a treasured "magic charm" in your life.

But What If I Am Successful?

Last, you might have fears about succeeding. In the first two lines of her poem, "Our Deepest Fear," Marianne Williamson states: "Our deepest fear is not that we are inadequate. Our deepest fear is that we are powerful beyond measure."[4] This fear usually has ties to a deeper terror of being seen, being persecuted, or being shunned for your brilliance. These fears and the rest I've shared are usually very old fears that are revealing themselves for the purpose of being healed.

We'll be tackling fears with a different set of tools in the next section of this chapter, but in the meantime, you can continue using the flash paper exercise to help release them.

Process Questions

➻ Articulate in your sketch/notebook what the previous three exercises in this chapter were like to perform.

➻ Think about how your feelings about yourself as a creative person may be shifting.

➻ What exercises do you imagine you'll keep practicing?

➻ How do you imagine you will continue to work with old fears to disable their hold on you?

➻ Record your impressions about these exercises so you can go over them again at a later time.

Be gentle with yourself as you work through your fears.

HEALING THE FEELINGS

There is a caricature in our culture of a creative person. You've probably read about such a character in books, seen him or her depicted in movies, and even seen the characters sing their hearts out in operas. If we were to create a recipe for this fictional personality profile, it might look something like this:

The Creative Caricature

Ingredients
1 cup brilliant ideas
2 cups feverish creative output
1 cup dazzling technique

Mix together and season well with:
¼ cup fits of melancholy
1 heaping tablespoon existential angst
1–2 pinches "no one understands my vision"

While there might be some person somewhere who fits this profile, it certainly doesn't fit most of us. That being said, all human beings, whether they consider themselves to be creative or not, are seasoned with inner emotional struggles.

Why is this so important to your creative life? That answer is simple. Your feelings can either enhance or shut down your creativity. The reason is that it all goes back to consciousness.

Consciousness has a role in the creation of our tangible reality and that consciousness is both thought and feeling. The most important part of consciousness is feeling, and I've already given you a tool to reset yourself when you are experiencing fear or one of its many faces, such as anger. However, now it is time to begin teasing apart repetitious feelings to find the patterns or treacherous thought loops that lie at their root.

Your feelings give you important information about your subconscious perceptions. In general, fears are lodged in the subconscious and are a product of our making decisions about ourselves and the world around us based on our early experiences. Until about the age of seven, a child has no way to discern the difference between the inner and outer worlds. Without adults who are healthy enough to realize this and willing to repair the child's misconceptions, the child develops perceptual distortions about the self and outer world. For instance, if something bad happens, the child may feel that he is responsible for it. If the world is chaotic, the child tries to create order in her world without the skills required to do so. This results in distortions of belief about who the child is, such as, "If I was good, Mom and Dad wouldn't be fighting," or "Daddy died because I was bad" Often, these are experiences we may have had during our preverbal infancy.

Even though you may have had such fears for most of your life, they can be healed. Identifying that they exist is a step. Realizing that they are a result of your misperceptions garnered in your early childhood can give you compassion about why you have them. Then you can begin transforming them when they intrude in your life.

A great way to begin rewiring the subconscious mind is to use the time before you go to sleep. Just before we go to sleep, in the delta brainwave state, we enter theta. During theta, the subconscious is more accessible. It is a perfect time to begin reshaping your subconscious patterns.

Lipton, the author of many books, including *The Biology of Belief*, has said: "We are not victims of anything other than the programs we are operating from. Change the programs you are operating from. If your subconscious programs match the wishes and desires of the conscious mind, your life will be one continuous honeymoon experience for as long as you live on this planet."[5] Make this a tenet you live by.

Reprogramming the Subconscious

For this you will need your sketch/notebook at your bedside to capture ideas or dream imagery that may have burbled up overnight.

1. Climb into bed and get comfortable.
2. Allow yourself to breathe deeply and restfully.
3. Just before you fall asleep, visualize and *feel* what it is you want to experience as if it is already accomplished.
4. Quietly speak aloud, saying, "I am grateful for [insert accomplished desire here]." *Choose just one,* and make it one that transforms your awareness of yourself and the world around you into one that is more supportive of who you are becoming. Some examples are: "I am grateful for feeling worthy," or "I am grateful for being able to love myself," or "I am grateful for the bravery to be myself," or "I am grateful that the world is a safe place for me."
5. Continue repeating this message in your mind until you fall asleep.

Do this nightly until you feel the old pattern or perception has been replaced by a new framework of thinking!

Once you have dedicated a few months to clearing your subconscious, additional reprogramming can be done as awareness of old material bubbles to the surface. I consider this clearing a lifelong pursuit, as we all have been affected by tens of hundreds of generations of negative enculturation. When something comes to the surface, use the preprogramming technique to address it. If some pattern of belief comes up that feels too heavy to handle with these tools, get extra support from a therapist. Don't ever be afraid of accessing the skills of these highly trained counselors. If you feel that you could use some help in unpacking and healing an old perception, find one you are able to see in person or use one of the new online therapy resources. As I like to say to my clients and mentees, "You didn't develop these fears and troublesome patterns on your own. You were affected by other people's beliefs and behaviors. So why should you have to heal them by yourself?"

In addition to supporting personal change, practicing this liminal state of awareness also will be effective as a part of enhancing your creativity.

Process Questions

- ●◆ Articulate in your sketch/notebook, as best you can, the bodily, emotional, and spiritual sensations of learning you can reprogram your subconscious.
- ●◆ Think about what new way of being you may want to add to your reprogramming effort.
- ●◆ Think about creating your own ceremonies to assist you in continuing that process of reprogramming. What would they be? How would they look?

If, in your process, feelings of anger arise about when and through whom you received your limiting beliefs, let yourself feel them fully. Then use the method I shared to release your feelings of anger or sadness.

Learn to be tender with yourself.

THREE

Nurturing Your Creative Brain

When discussing creativity, Michael Grybko, a research neuroscientist and engineer from the Department of Psychology at the University of Washington, says: "In science, we define 'creativity' as an idea that is novel, good, and useful. . . . [creativity] is very much a function of the brain. There's no need to invoke all that folklore into this. It's our brains doing what they do."[1]

Inside the brain, all of us have an extraordinarily complex net of specialized cells that continually transmit electrical signals. These neurons, or nerve cells, pass electrical signals to one another via neurotransmitters that chemically bridge the gap between the neurons.

The average human brain has about 86 billion of these neurons and many more glial cells that serve as a kind of scaffolding to protect and support the neurons in their ability to reorganize connections. Each neuron may be connected to up to ten thousand other neurons, passing signals to one another via as many as one thousand trillion synaptic connections, equivalent by some estimates to a computer with a one trillion bit per second processor. In other words, its processing speed is exceedingly fast. As to the size of its "hard drive," current estimates of the human brain's memory capacity are 2.5 petabytes, which is a million gigabytes.[2] Since the brain remains reprogrammable or plastic for as long as you are alive, your amazing organic computer is also capable of constantly improving its connections.

In addition to your brain, similar neural tissue is located in your heart and gut. These "brains" have made you an amazing information-processing organism capable of not only exploring the outer universe but also of reflecting upon the deepest aspects of your own self. *You are an extraordinary expression of the cosmos's infinite creativity.* Take a minute to let that idea sink in.

HOW IDEAS ARISE

Within your amazing net of neurons, an idea arises when a group of neurons in your neural net fires in sync with one another in a new, unique way delivering an idea to the conscious mind. Sounds simple, doesn't it? Well, fortunately, your mind, your living consciousness, is even more complicated than a complex processor and receiver of electrical information. While the brain is part of the visible, tangible world of the body, your mind is part of the invisible, transcendent world of thought, feeling, attitude, belief, and imagination. In other words, your mind is not confined to your physical substance.

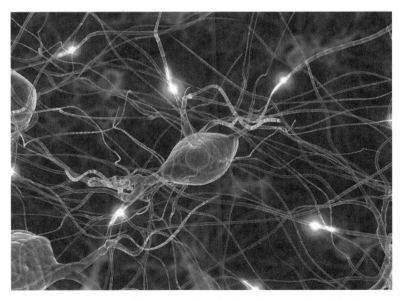

Your elaborate neural network is the hardware utilized by the transcendent mind to bring that which is intangible into form.

Two forces in our mind are necessary for survival but are also often at odds with one another. One aspect of our thinking is very linear. It is practical, logical, methodical, and analytical and pays attention to details. This part prefers predictability, structure, and safety but abhors change. It is an early part of the brain that is rooted in fear and is excellent at rationalizing why you shouldn't do anything differently. "Don't rock the boat!" it screams. "Don't diverge from the beaten path, or something bad might happen!" While this aspect of us may be helpful in true survival situations, it's also an ever-vigilant, inner Chicken Little who continually searches for evidence that the sky is falling. Sure, it's useful at reminding us that we need to attend to work and for doing linear tasks such as balancing the checkbook and making sure that we shut the burner off on the stove, but it can be a serious roadblock to living a full, creative life. Creativity, achievement, and growth all involve some degree of risk in that they require straying from the known path; in other words, exactly the sort of thing that causes the linear mind-brain to hyperventilate.

Part of the creative journey involves defying this resistance. To do that, the other aspect of our mind needs to be engaged. This involves the dance of quieting one aspect of our mind to allow the other aspect to step forward.

Thankfully, the rational mind naturally recedes every day. Daydreaming, imagining, or momentarily losing track of time are common examples of your linear mind taking a brief vacation. This linear mind also quiets down just before sleep and often takes a bit to go back online in the morning.

PUTTING YOUR RIGHT BRAIN IN GEAR

When your rational mind is off-line, the nonlinear, conscious mind steps forward. This aspect is often commonly referred to as the right brain, which is partially true.

Your brain is physically divided into two hemispheres, and although both hemispheres work together to perform cognitive tasks, it is generally thought that the right hemisphere is more visual and intuitive. In part, your brain's right hemisphere controls attention, memory, reasoning, insight, and, most importantly, problem solving, which are all critical aspects of creativity. Neuroscientists have learned this primarily through observation of people who have had right hemisphere strokes, which hamper these exact abilities. However, the nonlinear mind is connected to your entire brain's neural framework. It is emotional, spontaneous, intuitive, flexible, and abstract; has a high tolerance of ambiguity; is able to suspend ordinary reality constraints (thinking outside the box); and views the world in a big-picture way.

This is your wellspring of creative thinking, because in order to open up your intrinsic creativity you need to be able to view things in new ways or from a different perspective to generate new possibilities or alternative solutions. To have a robust right hemisphere, which is an essential part of your creative brain, you need to exercise it. When we learn new things, an electrical signal is sent down a neural pathway. Each time that same pathway is traveled, the sheath of myelin around those nerves grows thicker. This makes the transmission of the electrical signals faster and more effective. The effect can be compared to a single-lane country road that transforms into a robust highway simply because it is traveled more often.

Most of our educational training improves the rational, linear aspects of our brain and makes them robust. This prepares you to live a predictable, orderly, and rational life but doesn't support you to be flexible, innovative, intuitive, or able to flow with change. To have your creative energy flowing more effectively, it is important to get working on those right hemisphere superhighways.

IT'S NOT JUST THE CONSCIOUS MIND

The nonlinear aspect of the mind is in cahoots with the subconscious and therefore can be actively working while the linear mind is occupied, sleeping, or otherwise off-line. It is shaded by emotion and able to conceive of reality in a spacious, abstract, and unfettered manner. The nonlinear mind allows us to expand beyond the known horizons and experiment with new information and experiences. It is part of learning and growing and an essential element in creativity.

In her article "A Journey into Chaos: Creativity and the Unconscious," Nancy C. Andreasen suggests that the aspect of our mind that lies beneath waking consciousness operates under the parameters of chaos or complexity theory. This theory is the study of dynamic and nonlinear processes and of self-organizing systems. A self-organizing system is one that has many components and that organizes itself without a designated leader or central control. We can easily witness this action in nature while observing the movements of flocks of birds or schools of fish. In these two examples, we can see that the group of animals produces a form of organization that is distributed throughout the entire system and requires no centralized control.

Andreasen states that "[this form of organizational] system is dynamic, and changes arise spontaneously and frequently produce something new. Seen within this context, the human brain is the ultimate self-organizing system, and creativity is one of its most important emergent properties."[3] Simply put, your subconscious has its own kind of nonlinear brilliance that can provide flashes of insight and solve problems. In addition, this happens continually throughout the nonlinear creative process and requires no input from the linear mind to accomplish.

It is also precisely because the nonlinear mind is spacious and unfettered by the limits held in your ordinary linear mind that true creativity has spiritual and emotional aspects. The creative process works with unrealized potential, and the creator works collaboratively with that potential, as though it already existed. This is true even if the final result of the creative process produces something other than what was initially conceived. Being in relationship with formless ideas is crucial to the process, as is resisting the urge to prematurely form what is still intangible. It has similarities to the dance of courtship and exploration one would do with a person before becoming his or her partner or lover. If any step is missed or rushed, the relationship can falter, and in terms of creativity, the process itself could get shut down. A creative person must learn how to be comfortable voyaging into the unknown because all creativity is a process. You learn to coax the intangible idea and shape it while being in partnership with it.

In that way, you can also think of the creative process as having a spiritual aspect. During the process, a creative person engages fully with something, which at the time does not exist in the physical dimension. The artist, author, musician understands that the formless idea must be collaborated with and never forced into shape. It is a give-and-take with the intangible world and has parallels with how the shaman perceives the complex nature of reality as containing formless as well as fully manifested energies, which exist together on equal terms. In that way, the creative process has affinities with the journeys a shaman takes into the spiritual realm to negotiate with ethereal energies that impact physical reality. In other words, the creative person has some properties of the shaman, which is something I'll be expanding on throughout the book.

To better understand how the nonlinear mind works, we need to expand our exploration of the intangible and most powerful aspects of being human that lie beyond the mind—which is consciousness.

You see, your mind is part of your consciousness, but your consciousness transcends your mind.

DOWN THE RABBIT HOLE WE GO!

You are more than what you see in the mirror. Indeed, that reflection gives you the illusion that you are physically solid. Albert Einstein once said, "Reality is merely an illusion, albeit a very persistent one." I can't argue with Albert about that; however, our world seems so very concrete. We see it, taste it, touch it, hear it, so it must be true—but is it?

Contemporary physicists, such as Mark Comings and Amit Goswami, have been involved in exploring the foundations of physics through a number of innovative, elegant, and unconventional conceptual approaches. Comings's focus has been on the physics of space, time, light, and energy. Fundamental to this view, referred to as the new physics, is an understanding that matter—the stuff of our physical reality—isn't solid at all. In fact, everything is vibration.[4] All matter—our bodies, the elements, and everything that exists in our physical world—is first and foremost incorporeal. In that respect, the latest physics has a lot in common with the ideas of indigenous shamans. Whether we call that incorporeal essence, vibration, energy, or spirit, we are still agreeing that an intangible "something" is the basis for everything.

Our consciousness is also intangible, and yet, in spite of its ephemeral nature, its effects are profound on the material world. Indeed, consciousness is now thought of as a primary feature of our newer, quantum understanding of physics in that it is a participant in the creation of matter from vibration and its dissolution back into vibratory formlessness. Your individual consciousness and mine are part of the larger consciousness of ultimate creativity. Our individual consciousnesses may be thought of as a state, or quality of sentience, or awareness of internal or external existence.

Individual consciousness also has many levels. You have the ordinary consciousness of your day-to-day experience as well as the layers of consciousness that expand into your deep personal wisdom, memory, and knowledge that you possess, even if you are unaware of it. Beyond that, you are also capable of expanding into a high state of consciousness that is closer to the consciousness of ultimate creativity.

Most of us typically access only a small portion of our potential consciousness, leaving so much of our power untapped. People driven to explore the nature of their creative being are naturally drawn to a much broader, deeper, and more expansive experience of consciousness.

Consciousness itself is nonlocal in nature. In other words, it exists and functions outside the restraints of our ordinary, space-time reality. That means it is not limited to any particular point in physical space, nor is it limited by our understanding of time as a linear progression of moments. In that way, consciousness is an energetic continuum that occupies the very same sphere of reality—beyond linear time and space—that a shaman would refer to as "the spirit world." Consciousness just is.

The new field of quantum physics suggests that consciousness is a primary feature of physics. The quantum vacuum or quantum plenum is a field of infinite possibility filled with the primordial vibrations that produce the particles that constitute all physical matter. It is the source of everything that has, that does, and that will exist. This field of light is not only more fundamental than matter, it also supersedes space and time. The vibrational waves in it are forms of light. Of course, this is not simply the familiar light of the electromagnetic spectrum but what Comings refers to as a primordial, unifying "sea of radiance," in which everything exists. Indeed, Comings suggests that all matter—everything that we understand as physical—is actually a kind of crystallized or condensed light.[5]

The primordial light that encompasses All That Is makes the shift from formlessness into matter because of the light of consciousness.

In stating this, physicists are not referring to ordinary, everyday consciousness but rather the higher, expanded consciousness that human beings can access through the disciplines of meditation and in the shamanic state of awareness. Indeed, Comings suggests that human beings have an "indwelling light of consciousness." This description reveals the spiritual nature of higher consciousness, in that this aspect of our nature is both the light of All That Is and the action that is continually creating matter. In other words, light and consciousness are inextricably interwoven, and human consciousness is an intrinsic feature of the field of reality that has a critical role in not only physics but also the biology of all living beings.

With this idea, we can begin to understand our inherent creativity as the energetic aspect of our individual consciousness that participates in the making and remaking of matter. The more fully conscious and aligned we become, the better able our creative energy can manifest beautiful, healthy, and magnificent possibilities.

No matter how long I've understood that concept, it still excites me into a fit of delighted shivers!

THE EMOTIONAL SELF, CONSCIOUSNESS, AND CREATIVITY

Our continual emanations of consciousness throughout nonlocal reality can be thought of as our conscious and subconscious awareness that is fused with and influenced by feelings. When an individual becomes facile with maintaining an alignment of clear, focused thoughts and clear life-giving feelings, they become more able to enhance their natural creative energy.

Consciousness is not only what makes us who we are; in its highest expression, it connects us to the larger, universal consciousness that is continually remaking the cosmos. This intersection of our individual consciousness and the greater interconnected consciousness is the playground of creative energy. To take full advantage of the powerful potential of this state, you have to learn how to refine your consciousness's tangible effects on your inner and outer worlds.

To learn how to modulate the deadening aspects of consciousness and encourage the positive ones is a critical part of unleashing your full creative potential.

Indeed, creativity elicits many feeling states. When the flow is going well, it can be euphoric and at other times disheartening and disappointing. Indeed, I have experienced just about every feeling in my emotional repertoire when in the middle of a creative flow. Learning how to work with the inner technology of our feelings is beneficial to our creativity and also to our health and overall experience of life.

Below are two easy meditations to start the process. These are simple breathing exercises that can assist you in feeling calm and open you

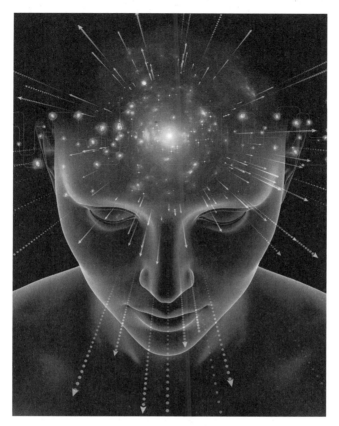

Your consciousness is multilayered. It is capable of growth, expansion, and feats that we are just beginning to understand.

to a more relaxed and expansive way of being. This is especially useful when learning new things. When we are learning something new, we are effectively challenging our current beliefs or understanding of the world. While having one's worldview challenged can be exhilarating for some, for others it induces a state of anxiety. This is because the linear mind's map of reality is being disturbed.

For some folks, the very word *meditation* creates anxiety. Intrusive or negative thoughts might arise such as: "What if I can't do it?" "I'll never manage to sit still that long!" Or even the dismissive: "Humph! Meditation is for [insert the speaker's idea of a frivolous person here]."

Truth is, you have an onboard technology for meditation. It is all about learning to intentionally work with what your body already has available to help you. These meditations provide ways of using breath to adjust the responses your body manifests. They do this by co-opting your body's natural calming processes to regain equilibrium. In other words, these meditations are ways you can hack into your nervous system's stress-relief system.

Your central nervous system is a complex array of neurons, all designed for a specific purpose. Sensory nerves provide the ability to perceive the world through your senses and also transmit sensory feeling impulses from your body's inner environment. Your ability to have physical sensations and to see, hear, smell, taste, touch, and feel are all part of the wonders of your sensory nervous system.

You also have a motor nervous system, which has two aspects. The somatic nervous system aspect of the motor system handles voluntary movement, such as walking, grasping this book, or moving the muscles of your lips, mouth, and throat to speak. This system gives us the ability to move our hand away from the hot stove our sensory nervous system warned us about.

The other aspect of the motor nervous system is the autonomic nervous system. That aspect handles involuntary muscle movements such as heart contractions, gut motility, eye blinks, gland secretions, diaphragmic motion we need to breathe, and other necessary life functions that we don't have to think about doing.

The autonomic nervous system also encompasses two aspects. The *sympathetic* division of the autonomic nervous system is responsible for the body's response to a perceived threat. This aspect of the autonomic nervous system is *not* driven by the brain. Its driver is located in the thoracic and lumbar regions of the spinal cord. That's roughly the part of your spinal cord that lies from your shoulders to your hips and is responsible for mobilizing the body's fight, flight, or freeze response. It makes the body tense, increases heart rate, contracts the muscles, releases adrenaline, and shuts down other functions of the body that it deems unnecessary in the situation. When you are stressed either by an actual circumstance, such as a car bearing down on you, or by an internal stimulus, such as worry, your sympathetic nervous system tries to help you by getting you ready for fighting, running away, or freezing like a deer in the headlights. Of course, the external circumstances that trigger the sympathetic nervous system response are far less likely to occur than the internal, never-ending litany of threats your mind continually creates. These thoughts arising from the unharnessed linear mind are damaging to the physical body and can lead to stress-related illness. This state also knocks your creativity out cold. You simply can't access your full being in this state.

Opposing this system is the *parasympathetic* division of the autonomic nervous system. It is largely responsible for the "rest and digest" aspects of life and originates in the medulla oblongata or brain stem; in cranial nerves 3, 7, 9, and 10; and in the sacral region of the spinal cord. This is you, from your neck up, working in concert with your spine's bottom terminus to keep you calm, present, and relaxed. It slows your heart rate, relaxes your muscles, and helps your gut process food more effectively. This system can counterbalance the agitation of the sympathetic response. You can easily remember the differences between these aspects of the autonomic nervous system by thinking about the parasympathetic as your *para*chute.

Breathing meditations that encourage a parasympathetic nervous system response can be really simple, involving a focus on the breath. You don't need any special equipment, just the ability to breathe through your nose. Nasal breathing is tied to the parasympathetic nervous system, but try both nasal and mouth breathing and see which one fits you best.

Don't worry if your mind wanders at first. These methods may be new to you, and the linear mind always squawks when we try something different from our usual routine!

The effects of these meditations are gentle and produce effects that support your overall health and well-being, not just your creativity.

As Easy as One, Two, Three, Four!

This is a very simple breathing technique for triggering a parasympathetic nervous system response to bring about calmness and relaxation. With practice, it can also assist in opening deeper awareness.

The method is to simply count to four, then count backward from four, all timed with your breath. Breathe in from your nose and out through your nose for best result. Do not hold your breath. Instead, breathe in a quiet but full manner while counting during your inhalations and exhalations.

> Breath in—count one
> Breath out—count two
> Breath in—count three
> Breath out—count four
> Breath in—count three
> Breath out—count two
> Breath in—count one
> Breath out—count two

Repeat this process of timing your breaths while counting to four forward and backward for at least fifteen minutes.

After you are through, sit a few moments and allow your entire being to reflect. If words or images come to you about the exercise, take some time to write what you experience during this meditation—without judgment—in your sketch/notebook.

If this exercise or any other in this book leaves you feeling spacey or ungrounded, use your five senses for grounding.

1. Touch: hold a favorite object, pet your cat or dog, or gently touch the leaves of a plant.
2. Taste: have a little snack of something with a pleasant, intense taste.
3. Smell: take in a pleasant aroma such as flower blooms, fresh ground coffee, or something else that smells delightful to you.

4. Hearing: use sounds around you to ground in the present moment.

5. Seeing: notice and then name the objects in your surrounding environment.

Then, if it is possible, step outside to be with nature.

Since not every style of parasympathetic breathing fits all people, I've included another version here for you to try as well. This following exercise is a bit more complicated; however, it comes to us from the Eastern yogic tradition and has been validated by many centuries' worth of success stories. As before, read the exercise all the way through so you can internalize how it works before you sit down to practice.

A word of caution: Practicing the following breathing exercise is safe for most people. However, as this one involves holding the breath, there are special precautions you need to follow. If you have a medical condition such as hypertension, asthma, COPD, or any other lung or heart condition, talk to your doctor before starting the practice.

Once again, if you feel ungrounded after this exercise, use the grounding methods provided above.

❧ Meditation:
Four In, Seven Hold, Eight Out

This is another yogic-style breathing technique that involves counting. This one is said to calm the nervous system so well that it can reduce anxiety and support better sleep. Give it a try and see what you notice!

1. Rest the tip of your tongue at the top back of your teeth.
2. To begin, inhale deeply, and let out a deep exhale, along with a big sigh or whooshing sound from your mouth.
3. Close your mouth, and slowly inhale through your nose for a count of four.
4. Hold your breath for a count of seven.

5. Exhale deeply and completely for a count of eight, being sure to let out a big sigh or whooshing sound.

6. Repeat this process for at least fifteen minutes.

As you did with the previous exercise, take some time to write what you experience during this meditation, without judgment in your sketch/notebook.

As you work with these breathing exercises, remember that stress is a health and creativity assassin. The more you can remember to shift back to your parasympathetic response, the better you're going to feel. These breathing exercises are a great start. *Take the time (because you're worth it!) to practice one of these breathing exercises three times a day for three weeks.* As you go along, notice the effects the exercise has on your attitude and demeanor.

You may notice that, once you have entered a parasympathetic state, you not only feel calmer but you also regain mental clarity. Of course, you may experience other benefits, including new ideas and insights in this state. Be sure to make notes about whatever comes up in your sketch/notebook. Use it to take note of shifts and changes that ultimately influence your creativity.

Process Questions

➻ Articulate, as best you can in your journal, the bodily, emotional, and spiritual sensations you experienced during the breathing exercises.

➻ Did you find one exercise easier than the other?

➻ What shifts in your body or mind did you notice as you practiced them for a while?

➻ Record your impressions about this exercise so you can go over them again at a later time.

Once you feel comfortable with switching your parasympathetic nervous system on through meditation, it's time to learn how to develop facility with the rest of your feeling technology.

USING YOUR BODY TO PUT YOU
IN YOUR RIGHT MIND

Giving your right brain a turbo boost during the day will not only greatly assist your creativity, it will also give you a greater sense of overall well-being by making you more mentally flexible and able to ride life's twists and turns with more facility. This can be done in various ways. Your body, because it is bilaterally symmetrical, can be used to give your brain a workout. Here are a few exercises using your senses for you to try. As with all exercises, please read the instructions all the way through before you begin. Be sure to make notes in your sketch/notebook about what you notice and what thoughts arise after each exercise.

Using Your Eyes

You can do this simple exercise anywhere with no special preparation. If at any point something feels uncomfortable, stop the exercise and quietly breathe.

1. Identify something in your right field of vision and one in your left field of vision.
2. Move your eyes to the right, and focus on the object you've chosen.
3. Breathe in and out gently through your nose.
4. Shift your focus to the left side.
5. Breathe in and out gently through your nose.
6. Repeat ten times.

An Alternative Method

1. With your eyes open, slowly roll your eyes from left to right in a circular motion without straining them. Do this action three or four times.
2. Repeat the same action with your eyes closed.
3. When you open your eyes, breathe restfully and calmly for a count of ten.

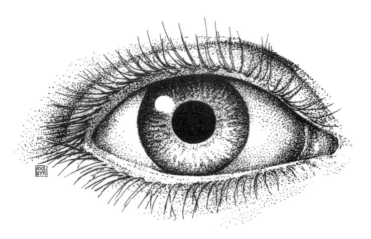

Our stereoscopic vision can support an easy way to exercise both hemispheres of the brain.

When you've completed the exercise, check in with yourself in your sketch/notebook. These simple exercises are very effective in helping to rev the right hemisphere and also for supporting the eyes to function well. If, like me, you spend a lot of time in front of a screen or doing what my grandmother would have called close work, it's very important to intentionally engage your distance vision. These movements exercise the eye muscles and also help to keep the lenses of the eyes flexible, which in turn enables your eyes to function better.

Using Your Ears

For some people, hearing, not sight, is their primary sense. Here is an exercise that uses the sense of hearing. Just as your eyes are connected to your brain's alternate hemispheres, so are your ears. This exercise uses sounds in your environment as points of focus. This exercise is best done while you are outside. As with the vision exercises, if at any point something feels uncomfortable, stop the exercise and quietly breathe.

1. Find a place to sit outside where you won't be disturbed.

2. Listen to your environment for a few moments.

3. Begin focusing on one particular sound on your left side. Listen for a moment.

4. Now switch to a sound on your right side, and focus on that. Listen for a moment.

5. Do this for a few rounds, and notice how your experience of your internal and external spaces feels.

6. When complete, make sure to process what you noticed in your sketch/notebook.

Now that you've utilized two senses, you may want to use physical motion to awaken the whole brain and balance it.

Using Your Limbs

This exercise utilizes walking and alternating your arms to awaken the right hemisphere and stimulate balance across the brain. If you have a physical limitation that would inhibit you from accomplishing this exercise, you may either skip it or try using your imagination to accomplish it in your mind. This internal method can be very effective as well, as the nerves in the brain fire exactly the same when we are imagining a task as if we were actually engaged in that action. (This is why I ask my students to avoid catastrophic thinking!)

1. Step outside.

2. Now begin walking naturally to relax and warm your muscles.

3. Once you have warmed up a bit, begin walking with your knees raised.

4. As you walk in this manner, touch your right palm to your left knee and your left palm to your right knee. This may feel awkward and may even make you giggle. Just do this until you have made at least twenty steps with each leg and palm.

5. Resume walking naturally, or simply stop and breathe.

An Alternative Method Using a Chair

Not everybody can ambulate easily. If walking is difficult for you, that doesn't mean you can't use your limbs to awaken and balance your brain. This similar exercise utilizes alternating limbs while sitting in a chair. Again, if you are unable to perform this exercise in a chair, use your imagination to do the same task.

1. Sit upright in a chair.
2. Touch your right elbow to your left knee.
3. Reverse and touch your left elbow to your right knee.
4. Alternate so that you engage each side twenty times.

Taking what has become an automatic task you take for granted and switching it up can really fire up your creative right hemisphere. The following exercise involves signing your name. Sounds simple, right? Well, let's try it in a new context.

Writing the Right Brain Awake

For this exercise, you'll need:

- A sheet of paper
- A mirror
- Your sketch/notebook and a pen

1. Sit at a desk or table with the paper and the mirror propped up nearby.
2. Sign your name on the paper.
3. Switch hands, and on the same sheet, sign your name again.
4. Now go back to your dominant hand, and sign your name but write it upside down.
5. Next, sign your name while only looking at the paper in the mirror.
6. Now, sign your name backward from the last letter to the first but so it reads correctly.
7. Sign your name backward.

8. Take a breath, and when you feel ready, jot down in your sketch/notebook what has come up in the process.

Whenever you practice this or other exercises in this chapter, you may find that your subconscious creative co-conspirator comes up with some interesting content for your sketch/notebook. Always keep it handy, as these exercises can produce some interesting thoughts and ideas. Even if you didn't initially feel inspired, your subconscious is taking this all in and will give you material to write or draw, even days later.

BREATHING TO OPEN UP CREATIVE FLOW

Breathing acts directly on the brain. Specialized breathing techniques that use alternate-nostril breathing have been well known since ancient times. The pranayama breath control process of hatha yoga is a good example.

Once thought of as solely in the realm of the spiritual and metaphysical, alternate-nostril breathing has finally been recognized by Western science as a natural way for the body to regulate the brain. Studies done in 1895 by the German physician Richard Kayser discovered that alternate-nostril breathing happens naturally and automatically during the day. Nearly a hundred years later, a 1994 study observed that breathing through alternate nostrils affected the brain's hemispheric symmetry.[6] EEG scans provided proof that this method of breathing lit up both sides of the brain and had a balancing effect on the functional activity of the left and right hemispheres. In other words, intentionally breathing through alternate nostrils activated the brain and caused it to be more balanced. Indeed, there are neurons in your brain that regulate the respiratory rhythm that are also connected to the part of the brain stem that is involved in attention, wakefulness, and your emotional state. Breathing can be a tool to calm down, quell anxiety, become more awake, be more attentive, and, of course, fire up the creative mind.

The following easy-to-learn, simple breathing exercise will help you to more fully engage the creative side of your gray matter. You may also do this exercise anytime to help make yourself more cognitively awake, positively attentive, and sharp.[7] Read through all the instructions before beginning the exercise.

A word of caution: if you have unmedicated high blood pressure, abdominal inflammation, a lung condition, a hernia, or any other medical condition that might be negatively influenced by holding your breath, omit that part of the following exercise.

Alternate Nostril Breathing

It's important to set up this exercise so that you won't have to focus on anything but your breath. To do so, you will need a straight-back chair, a table, and enough books piled up in front of you on the table so that your right elbow can rest on them at a level that makes resting your right index and middle finger above your brow easy—all while keeping your back straight. Fiddle with the height until resting your two fingers on your brow is an easy and comfortable position. You will be taking slow, smooth, steady, and relaxed breaths during this process. You do not want to force or strain your breathing. The pattern will be to first breathe in through one nostril and out through the other and then switch back and forth in a rhythm.

As always, have your sketch/notebook with you to write down whatever you may have noticed in this practice.

1. Sit in your chair.
2. Place the middle and index fingers of your right hand above the brow bone and rest them there. (You will be using your thumb to close your right nostril and the fourth and fifth finger together to close your left nostril.)
3. Close your eyes, and take a deep breath through both nostrils.
4. Exhale completely, and then use your right thumb to close your right nostril.

5. Inhale through your left nostril, and then close the left nostril with your fingers.

6. Open the right nostril, and exhale through this side.

7. Inhale through the right nostril, and then close this nostril.

8. Open the left nostril, and exhale through the left side. This is one cycle.

9. Bring your full attention to your breath as you follow this pattern of breathing. Continue this for five minutes. Always end with an exhalation on the left side.

Practice this exercise regularly to gradually build up the duration of breathing in this fashion until you can do it effortlessly for twenty to thirty minutes each day.

Work on getting comfortable doing this without the prompts. You'll find that by focusing on the breath and keeping your back both straight and relaxed, you will become able to do this exercise anywhere at any time!

This kind of breathing has many benefits beyond supporting your creative energy. Alternate nostril breathing, known by yogis and yoginis as *nadi shodhan pranayama*, has been shown to lower stress levels and improve cardiovascular functions. This way of using your breath as a wellness tool will also improve lung function and respiratory endurance. Focusing on the breath can calm your nervous system in the same way that meditation does, and performing this gently and slowly can assist in quieting the mind for better, more restful sleep.

As you can see, using your body, your senses, and your breathing can all help to awaken and strengthen the neural pathways in your brain that reconnect to creativity. You are in the process of becoming a truly awakened creative being. Doing this will enhance your experience of living and may even help you come up with the next big idea. I believe the quantum plenum is bursting with ideas just waiting for individuals to access and manifest. Keep focusing on making you and your beautiful brain fertile ground.

Process Questions

- ➡ How did it feel to work with your eyes, ears, breath, and body in this new way?
- ➡ What occurred inside and around you as you worked with all the different aspects? Was one exercise more potent than another?
- ➡ How did it feel to do the writing exercise with your name?
- ➡ At what times do you think you may want to use these methods in your daily life?

FOUR

Altered States and Creativity

Expanded consciousness can be explained as a state of elevated awareness in which we sense more than what is readily recognizable through the physical senses or is grasped by the rational mind. It is the heightened ability to directly perceive and experience subtle or profound truths and realities as they exist in both the subjective and objective worlds. In other words, it is a state of awareness whereby ordinary perceptions about internal and external reality are expanded so that new perceptions can be experienced and assimilated into a new version of ordinary. It is often accompanied by experiences of feeling a deeper connection with the living planet and the greater cosmos and an inner awareness of the divine.

We are wired for altered consciousness experiences. A study published in 1973 found that altered states of consciousness are virtually universal in their distribution across human societies. The study sampled 488 societies and found that fully 90 percent of them exhibited institutionalized, culturally patterned forms of altered states of consciousness. The study also concluded that the capacity to experience an altered state of consciousness was so universal that it seems to be part of the psychobiological heritage of our species.[1]

Author and journalist Graham Hancock, in an interview with artist Alex Grey on universal creativity, referred to the creativity that flows from this expanded state as being "open, not closed into a narrow reference frame. It's [a kind of creativity] willing to receive whatever is there, explore and develop it."[2] He further stated that creativity "needs to be open to any possibilities. Open to the possibility that the material realm is not the only realm and that we are part of a much wider, invisible, inaccessible totality." This kind of openness—of being able to access unlimited possibility and embody a part of it—implies not only a transitory experience of creativity but also of transcending thousands of years of limited perception and making an evolutionary leap in consciousness.

In chapter 3, I shared how consciousness is considered a primary feature of the new physics and thereby intimately joined to the universal creative energies that continually shape and reshape all matter. A growing amount of scientific literature suggests that expanded states of consciousness have enhancing effects on personal creativity. These studies are primarily based on the premise that people usually restrict their range of awareness and seldom exploit the more potent, powerful dimensions of their minds. That being said, it is clear to me that young children, those who have cultivated their creative processes, and those who intentionally expand their consciousness are *all* freed from these limitations.

Over my lifetime, there have been expansions of conscious awareness and perception, which have contributed to my own unfolding as a creative person. These experiences have been both spontaneous and cultivated, but in either case, they have given me sparks of insight—stretching my ability to hold more of what we call reality, which we now understand is the ever-evolving product of consciousness. These experiences were the *aha!* moments when suddenly my whole perception shifted.

The earliest and simplest of these occurred in childhood, before the age of three. The first moment I want to share is a memory I have from the autumn after my first birthday. I was toddling along a tree-lined sidewalk with my paternal great-grandmother on a warm and sunny fall day. It was the time of day when the low, honey-colored light of afternoon makes the turning leaves appear as if their colors were somehow being illuminated from the inside. As all kids do, I had picked up a leaf

One of my favorite pursuits each year is the search for the perfect leaf that epitomizes autumn.

on the sidewalk that caught my eye. It had a green stem and from there colors spread out to yellow through orange and finally to a deep red at the tips. It felt like all the colors of the season had been captured in one leaf. (I still look for one like that every fall!) I reached up to show my great-grandmother what I'd found, and she told me that she loved *maple* leaves, too. It was as if a bright spark blazed to life inside my head. Suddenly the trees lining the sidewalk became individuals with names, whose leaf shapes could tell me who they were. In that moment, my perception of the trees had made a leap: they were no longer anonymous, objectified *its*; they had become individual, specific *whos*. At that moment, I felt a rush of love inside me for those leafy companions that continues to this day.

A year or so later, I was sitting on the floor drawing things around me. We were done with reading for the day, as the adults were now busy with their own tasks. With crayons spread out around me, I had drawn a cup of coffee sitting on a table. Like most children, I had flattened the three-dimensional object so that all surfaces were visible in the drawing including the coffee inside. When I showed it to my mom, she smiled warmly and then asked me: "That's good, honey, but can you see the coffee in my cup where you're sitting?" Boom! No, where I was sitting the inside of the cup wasn't visible! In fact, from where I was sitting, the cup didn't look like a cup. The table edge blocked the bottom from my view, and the rim of the cup that was visible was actually curved downward. From that moment forward, I observed the world around me in a completely new way. I was no longer just looking at things but instead really *seeing* the physical world and how the elements of it interacted with one another and how my viewpoint altered their perceived relationships. Of course, I didn't have the language to explain all of that at three years of age, but that flash of insight became an essential aspect of my understanding.

In these childhood examples, it was if the lens of life widened to encompass a new perspective. Amit Goswami relates these moments with the idea of quantum discontinuity. Instead of a linear progression that would lead to the broader understanding, in quantum discontinuity a leap occurs that is completely out of sequence with the usual progression of steps. The resultant experience holds more than the

A shift of perception can revolutionize how you see the world.

original context, offering a much larger view that may or may not have been achieved through a linear progression of learning steps.

Anthropologist Gregory Bateson referred to this as Learning III, a state of mind that "reveals a world in which personal identity merges into all the processes of relationship in some vast ecology or aesthetics of cosmic interaction."[3] In other words, there is an experience of a larger context or a wider perspective and a deeper sense of connection that occurs during one of these moments.

Shifts that promote new ways of thinking about things and situations are a crucial aspect of creativity. These shifts can happen spontaneously, as in the examples I've shared, but it is vital that we also learn how to encourage expansions of awareness and nurture them when they arrive.

It is now thought by neurological and anatomy researchers that humans have a natural proclivity to alter consciousness and that this ability arose through evolution and contributed to our ability to adapt to change.[4] The knowledge gained in altered states, such as finding game or therapeutic plants, assisted in group survival. This ability may actually predate *Homo sapiens* and go back as far as *Homo erectus,* over two million years ago, as evidence suggests they were able to harness fire. They would have had nightly access to rhythmically pulsing firelight, which can trigger expanded states of consciousness.

EXPANDING CONSCIOUSNESS THROUGH THE USE OF FIRE

When you sit in front of a fire in deep darkness, the objects and people around you seem to shimmer and move in the flickering light. Firelight produces a stroboscopic effect in which darkness and light alternate rapidly back and forth. The rhythmic rate at which this occurs produces the same brain-wave states that are consistent with the experience of the shamanic state of consciousness. Since life revolved around the fire, our ancestors were exposed to trance-inducing fires every evening of their lives. They would have used this state to access the wisdom they needed for each new circumstance. In this state of awareness, they were able to look ahead and develop strategies for each new situation. It is part of what made them creative enough to survive.

What follows next is an exercise that uses fire to increase your non-linear brain's capacity through an experience of expanded consciousness and imagination. You will be staring into the fire for an hour or two with the intention of visiting the dark side of the moon. You will be sitting in a relaxed position, facing the fire, holding the intent to experience the moon and whatever you may find there.

Using Fire to Experience the Dark Side of the Moon

This experience can help open your visionary capabilities. For this exercise, you will need:

- A safe outdoor fire ring or indoor fireplace
- Tinder, kindling, and firewood for your fire
- Matches or another ignition source
- Your sketch/notebook and pen
- A safe way to extinguish the fire should an emergency arise

Choose a time when you will be able to spend a few hours with the fire until it goes completely out. Prepare yourself and all the materials before you start the exercise.

Performing the Exercise

1. Once preparations are complete, set your fire and light it.
2. When the fire is full, sit as close to it as you can safely, and gaze deeply into the fire. Allow the fire to create a dreamy feeling in you as you hold your intention.
3. Now envision yourself flying through space in a ship with an enormous spotlight on board, and close your eyes. The fire's flickering will still be noticeable through your eyelids.

4. Imagine that you are moving along toward the moon.

5. Once you are orbiting the moon, go to the side that never sees the sun.

6. Experience the darkness, and then turn on your spotlight to illuminate it!

7. Allow your imagination to provide as rich an experience as possible.

8. As the fire's flickering begins to die down, return your ship to Earth and feel yourself settle back into your place by the fire.

9. As the fire dies to coals, the flickering will stop, too.

10. Once the flickering stops, gently open your eyes.

11. As the embers cool, begin to record your impressions of the experience in your sketch/notebook.

12. When you are finished recording your experiences, secure the fireplace or extinguish the fire in the fire ring.

This exercise is one you can repeat often and is excellent preparation for the subsequent chapters in this book. Remember, if you feel spacey or ungrounded after this or any other exercise, follow the steps you have practiced for grounding in earlier chapters.

EXPANDING CONSCIOUSNESS AND CREATIVITY THROUGH ENTHEOGENS

Entheogens are psychoactive substances that induce any type of spiritual experience aimed at personal or transpersonal development or sacred use. These substances include DMT, mescaline, and other alkaloids, which are derived from plants, fungi, and some animals. In his essay "The Creative Process and Entheogens," visionary artist Alex Grey discusses the trajectory and potential stages of the psychedelic experience.[5] Grey believes his use of psychoactive substances has been critical in his own development as a visual artist with a higher mission. Examining the psychedelic experience is, I believe, helpful in understanding the creative process in general.

At the early stages of a psychedelic experience, there is a transition in which the outer world takes on a different quality. During this phase, the existing framework of perception is gradually released. This includes alterations in the usual quality of the senses and the manifestation of auditory or visual experiences that arise from the inner self. Depending on the psychological and emotional state of the person having the experience, these visions can be frightening or ecstatic.

A transpersonal phase follows this where the individual self is overcome. The higher self emerges, and with it comes a sense of union with the divine and a sense of superconnectivity with all life and the cosmos. This idea of a higher state of consciousness was proven in a 2017 study done at the University of Sussex. In the study, researchers used brain-imaging technology to measure the tiny magnetic fields produced in the brain and found that, across three psychedelic drugs, one measure of conscious level—the neural signal diversity—was reliably higher.[6]

In simpler terms, this experience may be distilled into a surrender of the ordinary, linear mind state to the nonlinear, spacious mind that inhabits the *liminal point*—the transitional space or threshold that defines the tangible and intangible, as well as the self and All That Is.

I would argue that this is also a perfect definition for the unrestricted flow of creative energy as it moves within a human being. However, creative energy is not restricted to an individual's experience of it. The energy river of creativity is a higher, unified consciousness in action, which we all have access to. When we fully open up to it and let it move through us, we benefit from it on a personal level. Allowing your own creativity to bloom can be an alchemical process that requires the release of your limited perspectives to produce "gold."

The benefits are on the transpersonal level as well. When we experience expanded states of consciousness, a new experience of self emerges that includes a transpersonal sense of connectedness. Surrendering to creative energy can transform your fundamental attitudes, perceptions, and understanding about yourself and the reality around you. As you continue to say yes to the transformative changes occurring inside while creative energy flows, you can become a more awake and active participant in the collective, unified consciousness's desire to benefit All That Is.

The late Ralph Metzner, psychologist and psychedelic researcher at Harvard University, wrote about the expansion of consciousness that accompanied the ingestion of psychedelic substances in this way:

> The process of consciousness expansion . . . was in some ways analogous to the process of awakening: when we awaken from sleep, our perceptual world opens up and we emerge from the closed cocoon-like state of dream and sleep to become aware of our body, the bed we're in, our sleep companion, the room, perhaps the garden outside the window, the greater world beyond—potentially all the way to the infinite cosmos. As we do, our sense of identity changes, we may remember the more limited dream world we had been in and find that we have a greatly enhanced freedom of choice—freedom to think and see differently, to move and do things that were hitherto impossible.[7]

In this way, expanded consciousness states dissolve the conceptual boundaries of ordinary expectation—unshackling the mind from enculturated limitations of what is into a state where one experiences the unlimited permutations of what could be. This is akin to the physicist's understanding of the infinite potential that underlies physical reality.

Experiencing expanded awareness can include a superlucidity where you consciously explore the hidden workings of reality while in the altered state. There can also be a flood of deep compassion, an awareness of transcendence, an experience of loving, as well as being love itself, and a profound sense of mystical union. In this way, expanding consciousness may be seen as a kind of heretical act. To be able to see, feel, and experience that which lies beyond our cultural paradigm means we develop the ability to change it. Yet it is not so much changed by our efforts but by us becoming an agent of the new. The visionary designer and architect R. Buckminster Fuller said it this way, "You never change things by fighting the existing reality. To change something, build a new model that makes the existing model obsolete." In this way, the expansion of our consciousness and the expression of our creative energy can become tools for the greater good—which I would argue is the ultimate role of the deeply creative person. Fuller certainly lived his life in accordance with this ideal. He thought of himself as a "comprehensive anticipatory design scientist" engaged in solving global problems. He became a role model for other architects, designers, artists, and scientists working to create a sustainable vision of our world.

It has been said that no change is possible without being able to imagine it first. Since the changes we are participating in as a species have never previously existed on Earth, it becomes necessary to have a tool by which we can have experiences of new possibilities. Igniting our imagination allows us to access the feelings of new possibilities, apply them in our feeling prayers, and finally manifest them. If we desire to create a new reality for ourselves, our entire species and the planet as a whole need to be able find that access to the new reality *before* it has manifested.

As our imagination expands with our consciousness, we can envision new possible solutions and ways of being.

While many of the examples I have shared thus far involved the use of hallucinogens, you do not have to use any illicit substances to have the same profound effects. Similar experiences have been achieved through deep, transcendental meditation, whereby an experienced practitioner becomes an individually aware self, experiencing him-, her-, or themself as omnipresent. In other words, the identity of self becomes more of what some might relate to the soul's experience of being aware of and yet not separate from the divine. The same kinds of changes have been reported by long-term practitioners of Eastern yogic traditions, or those rare individuals who have chosen to spend years in nature isolated from other human beings.

SHAMANISM: ACCESSING ALTERED STATES AND CREATIVITY

Shamanism has roots that extend deeply into our collective human past; evidence of it may be dated to over seventy thousand years ago. Originating in the time when people all over the globe lived as hunters and gatherers, shamanism is an ancient spiritual tradition that presupposes that the world around us is alive: plants, animals, rocks, water, and fire are filled with *spirit,* which enlivens and animates them. Furthermore, the health and strength of any individual being is a direct reflection of the vitality of this animating force. During the subsequent spread of our species to every corner of Earth, we carried this understanding of the world with us and incorporated it into different tribal traditions. Observers of widely diverse shamanic cultures—from Africa to the Americas to Asia—see amazingly similar practices that clearly reflect our common spiritual origin.

Shamanic Journeying for Tribal Survival

For much of prehistory, the usual human abilities of vision, hearing, toolmaking, and mobility were enough to solve the problems of daily survival. However, sometimes a need arose that was not as easily met by ordinary means. For instance, if several members of the tribal group fell ill, this would significantly impact the survival potential of the whole since each member was called upon to provide for the group. Yet why they were ill and how they could be made well was not something that could be known by using ordinary methods. What plants could effect a cure, and where did they grow? Another example might be the location of herd animals or migrating flocks when they were not in the local range. How might a band of human beings who traveled on foot be able to know in which direction to travel?

Knowing where the tribe could intersect a migrating herd, find a source of water, know what plants were safe to eat or could provide a cure, and other vital information for survival required the ability to gain insight from the invisible realms. To solve these essential riddles of survival, a member of the band needed to be able to expand her or his ordinary awareness to include that which was usually unseen, unheard, or untouched. The individual needed to leave the camp in a unique way, using spiritual eyes and ears to gather information, such as locating a herd of deer. Such individuals came to be known as *shamans,* and their *shamanic journeys* evolved as a tool for solving problems that couldn't be resolved using ordinary awareness or the five senses.

Traditional shamans believe that the spirit of any individual is capable of taking flight; that is, the spirit may partially leave the body.[8] This leaving and returning of the spirit is done intentionally by the shaman for the purpose of looking beyond our ordinary time and space reality. This is done to better interact with the numinous beings that enliven nature. While spirits are nearly impossible to see or hear with our ordinary senses, the shaman is able to interact with these beings easily by moving beyond his or her ordinary way of perceiving the world. Metzner wrote that

shamanistic and . . . Asian yogic traditions . . . [recognize] many levels of reality, many dimensions of being, equal in reality to the time-space-matter dimension, which is the only one recognized as real in Western science. . . . these . . . traditions also recognize the reality of

For our ancient hunter-gatherer ancestors, the shaman would have played a key role in finding the path of seasonally migrating herds.

beings, called "spirits" or "deities," existing in these multiple dimensions, that have their own independent, autonomous existence, and are not merely symbols or archetypes in human consciousness.[9]

When shamans enter the spirit world, they interact with their spirit helpers. These nonphysical beings exist beyond the physical world and are a source of healing, guidance, and wisdom. To be effective, a shaman has to develop a relationship with these beings. The shaman's spirit helpers function as companions, wise teachers, and interpreters of that which is as yet unknown to the shaman. They help the shaman to comprehend what lies beyond ordinary human understanding and then use that to shift, transform, or heal what is occurring on the physical plane.

Animal and bird spirits were often seen as teachers and guides that showed what was safe to eat, what water sources were available, and where the tribe might find shelter from the cold. As a result, early humans saw these creatures as companions and often as elder relations of the human family. These wise elder beings also partnered in the shaman's work. The animal spirits guided the shaman through hazardous battles with the spirits of disease, participated in negotiations with the game animals, and assisted in escorting souls into and out of this world, among many other tasks.

Of course, shamans do not relinquish their personal power to the spirits. Every individual is ultimately responsible for his or her own decisions. The input from the journeys simply provides the shaman with a different perspective and a broader view so that the shaman's actions and decisions can be as informed as is possible.

This intentional journey between the realms of the ordinary and non-ordinary realms is what defines a shaman and is the source of her or his strength, power, and ability to solve community problems. The shaman enters the realm of the spirits by expanding consciousness. The shaman's altered state of consciousness—or trance—may be induced through several time-honored methods, such as ingesting magical plants, sensory or physical deprivation, meditation, and exposure to flickering lights. Many cultures use some form of repetitive sound to expand awareness, such as prolonged dancing, rattling, chanting, or drumming. Repetitive drumming in particular is common to many different shamanic traditions.

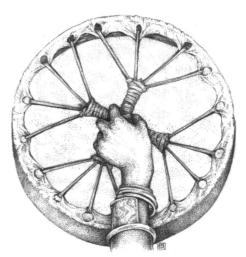

The sound of the shaman's ceaseless yet compelling rhythm opens a doorway to other perceptions of reality.

The Spirit World of the Shamans

Around the globe, the spirit world is described as a place. In essence, this world is both an actual place and a metaphoric representation of states of being that are not physical but rather outside both time and space. The shamanic journey, the act of leaving ordinary time and space or "walking between the worlds," separates the work of a shaman from other kinds of spiritual traditions.

Across the planet and throughout time, shamans have described the spiritual realms as having multiple levels. While the three realms indicated here are common, some cultures describe nine or more.

Typically, the consensual shamanic reality or spirit world is divided into three levels: the Upper World, Middle World, and Lower World. Some cultures perceive more than three separate spirit realms; for instance, in the Norse or Germanic tradition, there are nine realms. Each of these worlds can have many dimensions or levels within them. These levels are typically united by a central axis that it often described as a world tree, which can be used as a way to travel among the different worlds.

The Lower World is a realm beneath Earth characterized by a lush and vibrant landscape. It is filled with the spirits of animals, rocks, birds, plants, and those creatures that are extinct or those we think of as mythological. The Lower World feels primordial in nature. For instance, an animal in the Lower World feels more like an ancestor or spiritual template for the physical animals that live on Earth.

Passing through the sky accesses the Upper World. Many kinds of spirits are found on this level. The spiritual teachers found in the Upper World make themselves available to answer our questions, guide our steps, and encourage our own inherent inner wisdom. Like Lower World spirits, these teachers are safe sources of knowledge. These spirits, who have no need for a form, take a shape that is most useful for our interactions, which is most often humanlike in appearance.

The hidden reality of the world in which we live is called the Middle World. This realm is the place of physical manifestation. It is inhabited by all the spirits of the natural world, every kind of animal and bird, plants and trees, the elements, and the guardian spirits of nature Icelanders call the *Huldufólk* or hidden folk. These are the elves, brownies, nisse, *huldra,* faeries, greenmen, devas, and other similar beings who were honored by our ancestors as protectors and enliveners of the natural world.

The Middle World is also the place of physical manifestation, where the word is made flesh, where quantum vibration becomes physical matter. This refers not only to living beings but also to the energies of feelings, thoughts, and desires. For this reason, we need to be able to work both safely and with humility in this realm. The Middle World is where human beings have, in their unconsciousness, manifested the unbeneficial energies that need to be rebalanced. It is also where the disembodied spirits of the dead, negative emotional energy, and other spiritual and physical hazards reside.

Although the Middle World is rich with spiritual wisdom, journeyers need to learn to travel there safely and with discernment. For these reasons, it is necessary to make strong connections with protective, helpful, and healing spirits in the Lower and Upper Worlds before doing more work in the Middle World.

The next chapter guides you in shamanic journeys to the upper and lower worlds to enhance your creativity.

FIVE

Shamanic Journeying to the Lower and Upper Worlds

The ancient method of shamanic journeying is an awesome tool for stepping out of the linear mind state. Shamans and creative people function across similar landscapes in that they function in both the local and nonlocal universe—the visible world of our three-dimensional reality defined by our senses and the invisible worlds of energy, connection, and the intersection of universal or collective consciousness. In talking about the intersection of shamanism with creativity, Terence McKenna said: "The shaman is the figure at the beginning of human history that unites the doctor, the scientist and the artist into a single notion of care-giving and creativity."[1]

You do not have to become a shaman to use this method. Unlike deep meditative practices, shamanic journeying doesn't take decades of living in a yogi's cave to achieve results, nor does it require an entheogen or, indeed, any chemical stimulus. It is generally safe and easy for an average person to learn and offers access to the expansion of consciousness, which opens creativity. Using it can bolster your confidence, develop higher perceptual skills, and enhance your creativity, as well as develop new skills and abilities. In addition, the tool of journeying can open your mind and heart to unimagined possibilities and give you experiences of them that you can *feel*.

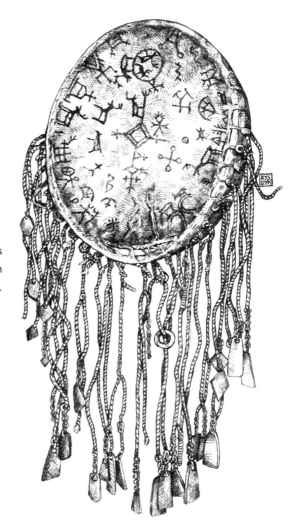

A Sami shaman's drum decorated with talismanic charms.

AN ANCIENT WAY TO ENHANCE
YOUR CREATIVE MIND

Since human perceptions about the nature of the world—what we understand as ordinary reality—are primarily based on the information provided by our senses, other ways of perceiving must be called upon to gain information about the unseen world. The shamanic journey offers the opportunity to intentionally expand our perceptions outside ordinary time and space for the specific purpose of gaining information, insight, or experiences that are normally hidden from us. It is these aspects of journeying that are so vital for stimulating creativity. The usually imperceptible energies that compose creation become palpable in an expanded state of consciousness. This wider view opens up possibilities that were not available before the shift in awareness.

Shamanic Journey Method Enhances Brain Waves

Along with shamanic journeying's ability to help us solve problems, find hidden information, and gain wisdom, the method produces a unique combination of brain-wave states that enhance creativity and intuition as well as improve cognitive abilities, such as memory, learning, and the ability to synthesize information. While journeying, our brains exhibit a symphony of waves, in the alpha, beta, delta, and theta range. With continued practice, these beneficial effects become more sustained even while in ordinary awareness.

Alpha Brain-Wave State (8–12 Hz)

Alpha waves are present when the brain is idling. It is the state you experience when you daydream or when you meditate. The alpha brain-wave pattern is related to a reduction of depressive symptoms and an increase of creative thinking. When your brain is producing alpha waves, you can also have experiences of mystical states of consciousness, and your right brain activity is engaged. The alpha state is hence more conducive to innovative thinking and the generation of new ideas.

Theta Brain-Wave State (3–8 Hz)

Theta waves are typically experienced as you drop off to sleep. In this state, you can experience deep reverie and have sensations of detached relaxation that can range from feeling drowsy to hypnotic-like states. You are also able to experience vivid mental imagery. This state is conducive to opening intuition as well as receiving inspiration and is another brain wave associated with increased creativity.

Delta Brain-Wave State (0.5–3 Hz)

Delta brain waves are the slowest and are generally experienced during deep, dreamless sleep. In this state we can experience a deep sense of connectedness to the universal and collective consciousness, of being inexorably connected in body, mind, and spirit to everything and everyone. We experience this state in the last part of fetal development, in early infancy, and in the last moments of our life on Earth.

Gamma Brain-Wave State (25–100 Hz)

Gamma brain waves are the fastest and relate to the simultaneous processing of information from different regions of the brain, a skill that is essential in creative thinking. They are also associated with heightened perception. This state facilitates the brain's optimal frequency of functioning with increased levels of compassion and positive emotions. These waves are associated with higher consciousness, psychic abilities, and out-of-body experiences.

Shamanic Journeying Enhances Right-Hemisphere Abilities

Through both strengthening the right hemisphere and supporting more connectivity between hemispheres, journeying encourages the entire brain to share information and so work much more effectively.[2] Arthur Koestler, in his seminal work on creativity, *The Act of Creation,* suggested that creative individuals not only have robust right-hemisphere abilities, but they also have a unique ability to translate symbolic or visual information into language and vice versa, called *transcallosal symbollexia.* In addition, they have the ability to synthesize or blend elements drawn from two previously unrelated matrices of thought into a new, meaningful form. This skill, called *hemispheric bisociation,* unitizes right-left as well as conscious-subconscious processes involving comparison, abstraction, categorization, analogies, and metaphors. In other words, this synthesis of right-brain and left-brain specialization produces an enhanced ability to live and work creatively.

All that being said, journeying is a great way to hack your brain! Not only does it support more right-hemisphere strength, it actually works so that the entire brain is working together. This makes you more creative and capable of original thinking and allows the subconscious to work in concert with the conscious mind. In that way, the shamanic journey process can help your creativity equipment to be better than it was before.

Imagination

Through imagination you can visualize something that doesn't yet exist. In addition, your imagination can help you to leave an idea open ended and so subject to additional modifications as new ideas emerge. We can only create new things if we can imagine them first.

Imagination is also a very useful tool for rewiring your brain. Your nervous system cannot distinguish between physical reality and a richly imagined one. As a result, the imagination can be harnessed as a tool for personal transformation. In many ways, your reality train runs on the tracks that the imagination lays down. Vividly imagining new possibilities for yourself are an important step in making them happen.

Synthesis

The ability to synthesize lots of material from disparate sources or from different regions of the brain is another vital skill for the creative person. Very few ideas are completely new; instead, most great new ideas are built on all that has come before. All the previous bits and pieces of ideas are churned and rewoven in a new and unique way that was never thought of before. For instance, a smartphone is a relatively new thing, but it encompasses all the things we were already using. The big idea was to house them together in a new, more convenient, and portable form.

Intuition

Your intuition is responsible for hunches and gut feelings. This aspect of creativity simply knows there is a solution; it just doesn't yet exist.

The intuitional mind is also the aspect that can give those spontaneous *aha!* moments that have not followed any linear thought process. Studies at Harvard revealed that the majority of presidents and managers of multinational companies attributed up to 80 percent of their success to intuition. In addition, your intuition is a way of distilling information via the automatic, instinctual, and often subconscious part of you. Open-minded, right-brain thinking is highly conducive to intuition, particularly in deep states of alpha.

Holism

This is your ability to think about or do more than one thing at a time, something that a creative person depends upon. This skill allows you to paint in one area of a painting while simultaneously thinking about the composition or even another project. One way this skill manifests for me is when I am writing. While I am engrossed in a topic, I may spontaneously get an idea for another book, a workshop, or talk that is completely off topic from what I am writing. When this happens, I smile, write the information down, and offer gratitude to that part of my creative brain that functions like an excited child who simply can't wait to share what she has come up with.

Visual and Visuospatial Cognition

Being more visual means being able to create a vivid, detailed mind picture of something that either may or may not yet exist. It also means being able to discern colors, shapes, and dimensions in clearer, more refined ways. Visual people also are able to recognize and decode patterns. While this skill might seem to be most useful for an engineer, fashion designer, visual artist, or architect, anyone can develop it to enhance his or her ability to recognize patterns of thought, motion, or behavior. Pattern recognition and understanding might be useful for a writer who is developing a character or a plot. It is also vital for a dancer choreographing a dance or for a guide or naturalist learning how to predict a shift in weather.

Your visuospatial cognition is responsible for your ability to imagine an object, to search for and locate objects in space, to shift spatial attention, to hold items in your visual memory, to mentally rotate an object, to make a larger shape by imagining or locating smaller components, and to understand differences and similarities between objects. (Those who can easily put together a complex piece of Ikea furniture have this in spades!)

Open-Ended Thinking

The more you allow something to evolve, as well as working actively on it, the better creator you become. It is a skill to be able to hold an idea or project with a light hand—allowing the more spacious nonlinear mind to participate more fully in the process. By doing this, you allow contact with your own unlimited nature, as well as tapping into the collective consciousness.

Ability to Problem-Solve

During journeying, one of the brain waves being expressed is tied to deep relaxation. With the mind in a more relaxed state and able to access its immense creative resources, it is naturally better disposed to deal with crisis and solve problems constructively. In addition, the activation of gamma waves produces more rapid processing of thoughts, ideas, and potential solutions.

Enhanced Ability to Learn, Implement, and Remember

Journeying changes in brain function can greatly facilitate learning and study. Learning becomes easier and quicker, and new information is more easily integrated into an existing knowledge base. This integration allows the newly learned information to be readily available for implementation.

Memory is also improved by journeying. Both retention and recall become enhanced. This may be a result of the fact that journeying fires up wide areas in the brain. Memory is dependent on strong and broadly spread neural networks. When you persistently activate neural synapses, they become more robust. This is termed long-term potentiation (LTP). In other words, you make an internal computer with a faster processor, more working data memory, and a huge hard drive.

Stress Release

The alpha brain-wave state has another built-in fringe benefit in that it actually releases accumulated stress and tension from both body and mind. In our hectic lifestyles, this makes for a more harmonious state of being and improved health and well-being, as well as offering other long-term benefits. As tension is released and stress is reduced, the creative mind becomes more able to free-associate, to synthesize information and come up with new ideas.

Ability to Implement Personal Changes

The shamanic-journey-enhanced brain also facilitates changes in disposition or attitude, enhancing constructive traits and eliminating unconstructive ones—catalyzing new awareness at deeper subconscious levels of synthesis. In addition, a creative mind can find new, exciting ways to approach the changes you desire.

Connection and Negotiation

Being able to build rapport with others and develop harmony among people is a skill that can mean the difference between agreement and nonagreement, deal and no deal. Being able to connect and then support harmony among members of your family, friends, or neighborhood can make for a more peaceful and enjoyable life.

Journeying to Recover Health and Balance

Based on my more than thirty years of working with people using the shamanic journey, I have seen that this process can be invaluable in helping you to recover your health and balance in cases of personal trauma, behavioral issues, and illnesses or emotional, mental, and physical pain.

Through experiences in the shamanic journey, you can have the opportunity to discover your own abilities to obtain extraordinarily practical and wise answers to important personal questions, overcome inhibitory fears, and acquire self-confidence and incredible heartfelt wisdom. This can support an experience of personal empowerment and a newfound joy in existence.

Much of the malaise people experience in our contemporary world seems to originate from the perceived disconnection of our bodies, minds, and spirits. The greatest gifts the shamanic journey can offer are ways to access your own innate wisdom while recalling your profound spiritual connection to All That Is. Through relationships with helpful and healing spirits and with the spirits of nature, you can develop a deep, unshakable understanding that you are no more or less important than any other being in creation.

As you remember your relationship with All That Is, perceptions will shift about who you are, why you are here, and how you can participate in the larger collective. We create our understanding of what is real based on our perceptions of the world. As your perceptions shift and change, your experience of reality will be altered, leading to genuine, concrete changes in life.

This holds true because most of what we know about the world is learned information. The very first education we receive is from the family in which we are raised and later from the larger culture in which our family exists. In other words, each of us was taught our conscious and subconscious definitions of reality. This process affects how we understand the world and ourselves. As we learn new definitions, we are capable of replacing our previously learned views with a more harmonious way of knowing.

This has immeasurable value as we can sometimes bump into cognitive resistance, especially while in the process of change. This resistance is the linear mind's inability to overcome a preconceived viewpoint or visualize that an object or problem can have more than one function or solution. In other words, the linear mind begins an isolated, internal analysis of why something simply can't work.

As you connect more deeply with the inner self, with the world of the spirits, and with nature, you unlock the grip your habitual patterns of thought have over you. As this happens, the limiting beliefs that were taught in early life will begin to fade away, allowing for new, healthier ways of being to arise. Simultaneously, you also gain indisputable personal evidence to act as an antidote to the compartmentalized and isolating conditions that have become so prevalent in our world over the past few centuries. I would argue that the amazing tool of shamanic journeying that our ancient hunter-gatherer ancestors used to achieve expanded states has never been more needed than now.

Going Beyond Sensory Perceptions

We have defined what we see, hear, and touch as reality. However, what we see with our eyes is only a tiny portion of the electromagnetic spectrum that we call visible light. Raptors, such as hawks and eagles, and some other animals see below red into the infrared part of the spectrum and can spot the heat trails left behind by their prey. Most insects, many fish, amphibians, reptiles, and birds, and even some mammals such as rats and mice can see the higher frequency of ultraviolet light. Our hearing only picks up a small range of audible sound, whereas elephants and whales can perceive below that range, just as dogs, bats, and other creatures can perceive far above it.

Determining what is real using sensory stimuli has intrinsic flaws, as all of the input we use to define that reality is secondary information. If you are looking at an apple, you are not seeing the apple. Instead, your eyes perceive the light that has reflected off the apple, traveled to your eye through its lens, projected onto the retina, and then been converted into electrical information that the brain tells you is an apple. The same is true about other sensory input. For instance, while I can bring my two hands together in a clap, and my nervous system can detect the sound of the collision, the sight of them coming together, and the feeling of my hands touching one another, the atoms of one hand never touch the atoms of the other. Nor do the atoms in one hand actually touch one another! The sound made by the apparent collision of my hands traveled through the air into my ears where it was also transformed into electrical impulses to be interpreted by the brain as a sound.

These examples help you to understand that our idea of reality is based on very limited sensory information, which has been transmitted, transformed, and then reassembled in our brains. Looking at reality in this way helps to free your mind to explore what lies beyond your sensory-programmed, ordinary consciousness.

For you and me to actually create a new reality, we need to *feel* that which we haven't yet experienced. To do this, we need a tool that can take us beyond our current experience of reality. We need to be able to enter the place that science calls the nonlocal universe. Shamanic journeying provides the context within which we can receive the information, guidance, and insight we require. The information we receive is often given to us as metaphor to help us grasp that which wouldn't normally be easily understood. Since our minds have no easy way to relate to what is beyond the three-dimensional world, the journey experience provides a kind of interface or bridge between our ordinary, waking reality and a timeless and formless reality so that the mind can assimilate information from the numinous world.

While journeys may be thought of as metaphoric experiences, they also produce actual and concretely useful information. As with all nonlocal phenomena, the nonlocal action is immeasurable, but its effects can be both tangible and quantifiable. They are as real as our nervous system's creation of all the sensory input we have received over our lifetime that we think of as ordinary reality. It is why we used the expression *nonordinary reality* to describe altered or expanded states of awareness.

As noted earlier, journeys are accomplished by using repetitive rhythms, such as repetitive drumming, rattling, chanting, or dancing. It is also useful to close off or diminish our ordinary sight with a blindfold or other screen so that our inner vision or "strong eye" (clairvoyance) can become more prominent. You may also get your information in a journey through inner hearing (clairaudience), through feelings and knowing (clairsentience), or combinations of the three. While I am more visual with hearing secondary, my partner gets information through feelings. We have journeyed simultaneously for our clients for thirty years. Although the information came to us in different ways, we have never had a discrepancy between the information we received. In other words, trust how *you* perceive in the journey state.

Learning the shamanic journey process* is fairly simple, but it is only through practice that the real benefits emerge. What follows are a series of exercises for practicing this method, beginning with finding your power animal. Shamanic journeying is one of the best ways I know to rewire you to be more creative and to more fully unlock the power of your nonlinear, spacious mind. *Each shamanic journey requires a razor-clear intent, a willingness to step outside your ordinary perceptual landscape, a trust in yourself, and a trust in helping spirits—with whom you have been nurturing a reverent, participatory relationship.* Take each step and fully digest it, and practice each one before you move to the next. Please don't hurry the process as you go along. Journeying can become an extraordinarily powerful, lifelong resource, so it is best to bring your curiosity and patience to the process. As you begin to feel its benefits, you will be glad that you took the time to develop this skill.

WORKING WITH A POWER ANIMAL: LOWER WORLD JOURNEYS

When a shaman goes on a visionary excursion, a guardian spirit in the form of an animal or a bird typically accompanies her or him. These

---

*There are many sources available for learning more about the shamanic journey process, such as books, audios, and even teleconferences. Toward that end, you may want to read my book *Spirit Walking: A Course in Shamanic Power.* However, if it is possible, the very best way to learn is to seek out a skilled teacher who can guide you. A good resource for finding a teacher is www.shamanicteachers.com.

guardians are called power animals. A power animal is different from the animal spirits of the Middle World, being a transcendent spirit that is a teacher, guide, protector, and companion for the shaman. For this reason, I often begin teaching people journeying by supporting them to meet a power animal.

These spirits remind us of a primordial time when people and animals were more closely connected. In her essay "Rock Art and the Material Culture of Siberian and Central Asian Shamanism," Ekaterina Devlet explained that "a common belief throughout Siberia is that in the mythical, timeless period 'before' the remembered time of human beings (a concept somewhat akin to the so-called Dreamtime of Australian aborigines) there were no distinctions in form or essence between people, animals and birds."[3] Furthermore, there is also a common belief throughout Siberia that when shamans step outside ordinary time and space to enter into the timeless world of the spirits, it gives them access to this deep, ancient kinship bond.

Ralph Metzner also shared a marvelous secondary benefit to working in the journey state with an animal guide, stating:

> Many individuals who have worked in a respectful and spiritual way . . . with animal spirit guides, have reported increasing communication from the spiritual realms of Nature in response to their divinatory questioning. Their messages and visions have to do, as one might expect, with practices that reduce our adverse impact on ecosystems, with the preservation of wilderness and the essential diversity of life, and with the development of sustainable, bioregional economies and communities.[4]

Metzner's comments are based on the understanding that shamanic journeys produce a transpersonal state of consciousness in which an individual's sense of self extends beyond the personal experience to encompass other beings, nature, and the wider cosmos. This expanded viewpoint encourages a sense of connectedness that is more pronounced than during an ordinary state of awareness. The expanded state also provides the journeyer with profound visceral and emotional feelings of being part of something larger than her- or himself. These feelings often translate into a deeper sense of caring toward other beings and of nature as a whole. This is also a prevailing motivation in the world of art, music, and literature. The images that touch us, the music that moves us emotionally, and the stories that stay with us for a lifetime all elicit an emotional response that takes us beyond our ordinary experience.

A shaman's power animal is a source of protection and guidance. The shaman honors the animal or bird in various ways, such as attaching talismanic representations or fetishes on his or her regalia and drum or by wearing a mask representing the power animal.

Power animals may take the form of an animal, bird, or mythic creature. As in the time when no real differences existed between humans, animals, and birds, power animals have the capacity to shape-shift into human form. In the same fashion, the time- and space-traveling shaman is able take the shape of a power animal. This shape-shifting is a merging transformation we will discuss more fully later on.

A shaman's power animal is an important source of protection. It is a steady companion on your life journey and can provide you with its transcendent wisdom and guidance as well as perform healings on you.

Developing a strong relationship with a power animal will strengthen your personal sense of being connected to All That Is. In addition, through relationship with this spiritual companion and guide, you will be able to safely traverse all the shamanic realms. With the steadiness and guidance these amazing beings provide, you will be able to step between the worlds with confidence. As you progress through your studies, you will learn to merge with them during any situation to augment your own personal power. However, before any of that, you will need to meet and get to know each other.

Meeting Your Power Animal

For this first exercise, you need to identify a place in nature where you feel safe. I suggest that it be a place that holds deep feelings for you, such as awe, wonder, peace, or some other feeling that has left you feeling grateful. This can be a magical place from childhood, a favorite place you return to often, or a place where you found solace or feel nurtured in some other way. You'll begin by getting comfortable, covering your eyes, and allowing yourself to remember this place in as much detail as possible. You'll want to remember how it looked, felt, smelled, and sounded, immersing yourself into your place as if you were actually there.

Then you'll start a twenty-minute shamanic drumming track with a callback signal, called "Shamanic Journey Drumming," an audio file of rhythmic drumming to assist you in your journey (available at audio.innertraditions.com/shacre). As you listen to the drumming, allow yourself to experience your place even more deeply.

After a few minutes look for a place to travel downward to the Lower World. A friendly animal or bird often appears to assist in your travels to the Lower World. Hold the intention to meet your power animal. Once in the Lower World, you will find yourself in a landscape that is often described as a primordial version of nature, where all creatures that have ever lived and mythical beings such as dragons or unicorns coexist. A power animal may present itself immediately, or you may have to wait a moment or two. When you meet an animal, ask if it is your power animal. You will sense an answer. If it isn't your power animal, ask it for help in finding yours. If the answer is affirmative, then greet this new companion and get to know it. Stay with this being until the drumming changes. Then retrace your steps back to your starting place. Have your power animal assist you in returning. This being will be available anytime you journey as a guide, teacher, and nurturing presence.*

A journey is incomplete without the return to ordinary reality. Retracing your steps at the callback is essential, as shifting into the expanded consciousness state and back to ordinary states of awareness is part of what helps to enhance your creative brain. During the journey, a shaman receives information and guidance and then retraces his or her steps to return fully to ordinary consciousness to implement what she or he learned. In a shamanic society, the tribe does not benefit if the shaman does not come back with a message, guidance, or healing method that is needed.

Furthermore, to *remain* in the world of spirit does not benefit *anyone*, as the shaman is jeopardized. In the shamanic view, when the spirit does not fully return to the body, illness can result and, if the entire soul is lost, even death. The people who go into the other worlds and do not return, whose psyches remain disassociated, risk both physical and mental illnesses. What separates the madman from the shaman, therefore, is *intentionality.*[5]

---

*Learning how to work with your power animal as a protector and support for you in ordinary reality may be found in my book *Spirit Walking: A Course in Shamanic Power.*

Your intentionality begins with a clear understanding of all the steps of the journey before you undertake your first experience—and the first step toward a safe practice is realizing that it isn't how far you go, it's how fully you return. Simply stated, this act of moving in and out of the visionary state is a major part of what defines the shaman and what will support the enhancement of your creativity.

One more note: you do not have to accept the idea of spirits to get the mentioned brain-boosting benefits from this process that I expounded on earlier. As yet, science cannot explain if it is spirits that we meet or our own expanded consciousness that produces the imagery, sounds, and feelings during visionary states of awareness. Either way, the process just works.

This exercise is best done when you are rested and alert. Please read through the directions carefully several times and gather all that you'll need before you begin.

Note that this exercise and several others in this chapter and the next all require you to sit or lie down in a comfortable safe place with a blindfold or bandanna covering your eyes while listening to "Shamanic Journey Drumming." If you are more comfortable standing or moving, you may do so to help you feel more inspired, both prior to and during the journey. Make sure you will be safe if you move around. Lift your blindfold slightly onto your brow so that you can partially see your environment.

For this exercise, you will need:

- A comfortable place to sit, lie down, or move safely
- Your sketch/notebook and a pen
- A blindfold or bandanna for covering your eyes
- A way to listen to "Shamanic Journey Drumming" (for example, your smartphone and headphones)
- A small snack to eat and a glass of water to drink when the journey is complete

Making the Journey

1. First, situate yourself in your comfortable place and in a comfortable position with your blindfold over your eyes. Put on the headphones, and

have the recording ready to play, but do not start it yet. If you prefer, you may rattle or drum along to the recording. The drumming rhythm and rate will help you to expand your awareness into the journey state more easily.

2. Take a few minutes to breathe deeply and remember something that fills you with gratitude.

3. Once you have gotten yourself fully into gratitude, allow your memory to take you back to a magical place you remember and a place where you felt safe. These are often places in nature we have felt to be sacred.

4. Filled with the strong feelings of that place, begin the "Shamanic Journey Drumming" audio file. While listening to the drumming, engage all of your senses in being in your special place. Notice as much as you can. What time of day is it? Where is the sun or moon? Is there a breeze or is it still? Are the scents of flowers, the ocean, or pine trees present? What is the ground around you like? Be as fully present in this place as you are able. Continue to explore. Get to know the trees, stones, and plants of your power-filled place.

5. Look for a place where you can go down to the Lower World. This can be an animal burrow, a cave, or some other opening in the earth. You may even also sense the great tree that unites the worlds. Keep holding your intent until you find a way downward. When you do, enter it and travel downward to the Lower World. You can ask a friendly animal or bird in the Middle World to help you go to the Lower World.

6. Enter the opening with the intention to travel downward into the Lower World to meet your power animal. Keep going down through the passageway until you come out in a landscape.

7. Continue to repeat your heart's intention about meeting the spirit of your power animal. Feel it already accomplished, and while doing so, use all of your senses to look for an animal or bird that is revealing itself to you.

8. You will know when you meet a power animal by noticing an animal or

bird that stays close. It may even be the one you met in Middle World that reveals its true nature to you. The animal may greet you, speak to you, or make some other strong form of connection. Be persistent until you meet.

9. Continue getting to know your power animal. Ask if you may embody your animal's spirit, and ask what the animal would like in return for its protection. Keep learning more about this spirit until the drumming changes to the callback signal.

10. Once you hear the change in the drumming, thank the power animal for being with you and for sharing its power with you.

11. Retrace your steps back to your starting place. As you do so, you will return your awareness to ordinary reality.

12. When the callback is finished, take a deep breath, and gently remove your headphones and blindfold. Open your eyes.

13. Enjoy your snack and glass of water to more fully return to ordinary reality.

14. Take some time to savor the experience and to understand all that you were given. Allow your heart to receive the gifts and write or draw in your sketch/notebook all that you have experienced.

If you feel vague or ungrounded after this or any of the other journeys in this book, go outdoors and feel the breeze touching your face. Then focus on your feet, and allow yourself to really feel that you are standing on the body of Mother Earth. Notice any trees, plants, animals, or birds that may be around you. Take deep full breaths and celebrate that you are alive in this moment.

If you didn't meet a power animal initially, don't worry. This kind of work can take some time. Be persistent and keep journeying to the Lower World until you do. Indeed, once you meet this being, you'll want to make numerous journeys to it. This being will become a protector, teacher, and healer for you. The time you take to meet and get acquainted with this spirit animal will be well worth it.

Process Questions

➻ What was the strongest aspect you noticed about your power animal? Did it have claws or wings? What were its eyes like?

➻ How did you receive information from your power animal?

➻ Notice the emotional feelings and bodily sensations that you had when you were with this being.

➻ Did negative feelings intrude on your process? If so, what were they? Write them down and see if you can get in touch with their source inside you.

Keep records of what you experience during your journeys so that you can refer to them at a later time. As you continue practicing this exercise, note what you realize about your own process.

Once you have met a power animal ally, it is important to do journeys for the purpose of getting to know your guardian. You are in the process of getting to know your power animal and developing a power-filled relationship. Let your power animal show you around the Lower World. Get to know how it communicates with you and how you are able to understand each other. Be compassionate and gentle with yourself as you learn and practice journeying to your power animal until you feel truly connected with this wonderful being. Again, let go of any ideas that you're just making up what you experience. I doubted this process in the beginning; however, over the years I found that it provided useful information and transformed how I am able to think and create.

Power animals can answer questions in your journeys, too. Indeed, for the first six months that I journeyed, I only met with my power animal. My animal ally provided wonderful insight and taught me things that still resonate with me over thirty years later.

The kinds of questions that work best in a journey are quite simple. They follow the "how, what, where, why, or who" format. In that list, you'll notice the absence of the word *when*. That is because you are stepping into the consciousness state that is outside our linear understanding of time. In addition, simplify the question so that it only has one part. I'll give you an example. Your nightly weather report said there is a possibility of seeing the aurora borealis in your area, and you want to know the best place to view it (something we like to do during a Maine winter). You wouldn't also ask for directions in the same question. However, you could get both pieces of information by asking a question such as: Show me *how* to arrive at the best place to view the aurora borealis. This way the question is simple and straightforward but includes all that you want to know.

Here is another example for how to phrase a question. You have a new employment opportunity, and you want to know what it would be like to be in the job and if it's right for you. In that case, you might ask something like: What question do I need to ask the employer that will provide the clearest information about this possibility? Of course, you can always journey repeatedly on a big issue, asking a different question each time. I like to do that when the area of inquiry has high stakes or consequences. Using the employment example, you might choose to make several journeys with questions such as:

How will it feel to do this job?
What are the consequences of accepting this position?
What is the right job for me?

If you are confused and having difficulty making a choice, you may want to ask questions such as:

Why am I feeling this way?
How can I get clear about [situation/person of concern]?
What is the best path for me to take to [achieve my goal/resolve my problem]?

If you need steps, as in a process or a recipe, ask: What are the steps to [making/doing something]?

As I tell my students, crafting the right question is the most important part of beginning a journey. You can see from these examples that each of these journey questions offers a shade of meaning that can help to clarify a situation. It is important to winnow down what you want to know into the simplest question, and that process also helps to clarify your own mind about what is most important to know. As with all journeys, return fully to this reality so that the deeper benefits of journeying will manifest.

Asking a Question of Your Power Animal

Refer to the exercise "Meeting Your Power Animal" for the list of what you will need to perform this exercise (see page 115).

Making the Journey

1. Get clear about your question, and write it down in your notebook.
2. Situate yourself in your comfortable place and in a comfortable position with your blindfold and headphones on.
3. Take a few minutes to breathe deeply and quietly and get into a place of feeling gratitude.
4. Once you have gotten yourself fully into gratitude, allow your memory to take you back to your special Middle World place, and begin the "Shamanic Journey Drumming" audio file.
5. Repeat your question at least three times as you make your way down to the Lower World. Let your heart announce your intention to the spirits.
6. Meet and greet the spirit of your power animal and ask: "Are you my teacher for this journey?" If the power animal isn't the one to answer your question, ask it to take you to a teacher who can answer your question. Before you ask your question, remember to ask the new spirit: "Are you my teacher for this journey?"
7. Once the power animal or teacher lets you know it is the one to answer your question, ask your question. Allow the power animal or teacher to answer. If something it says or does doesn't make sense to you, ask for clarification until you understand.

8. When you hear the drumming change to the callback signal, thank the spirits, retrace your steps, and return to your starting place.

9. When the callback is through, take a deep breath, and gently remove your headphones and blindfold. Open your eyes.

10. Partake of your snack, and drink the glass of water.

11. Record your experiences in your sketch/notebook.

Over the next few days, take several journeys to your power animal. During this time, ask new questions, have it show you around the Lower World, and do what feels right to deepen your connection. Building this relationship is vital as you move deeper into expanding your consciousness. A dependable guide is not only necessary but also comforting when you begin sailing off your usual map of how you understand the world.

Process Questions

- What was it like to ask questions of your power animal?
- How did you receive your answers? Make a record in your sketch/notebook of how you perceived the information.
- Did your questions lead you to want to ask more questions on the subject? Write those questions for future journeys.

Merging with a power animal is a skill that all shamans use to protect them while traveling through unknown territory. It is a type of shape-shifting, where a shaman would become a spiritual hybrid. In this way, the human shaman would be fully protected during his or her work. Reciprocally, the animal spirit would be given opportunities to experience the physical world—to be able to move, sniff, eat, and otherwise relish the delights of the body—as a part of its cooperation with the shaman.

Merging is also a way to expand what is possible for you to do in both the journey state *and* in ordinary reality. When merged with your power animal, you are in a spiritual partnership that can positively affect your ability to perceive the best action in a situation, to bring

Inuit sculptors have made images of shamans transforming into their protective spirits for many years.

you more strength for a difficult task, to nurture an even more profound connection to the natural world, to feel safe when you are blazing new trails, and so much more. It involves a blending of energies, consciousness, and on some occasions an actual change in physical form. I think of shape-shifting as a kind of joyful surrender of my ego so that the power animal and I both become something *more* for a little while. There is a magical quality to the experience.

Since we are one with everything and being, the kinship developed with a power animal allows you to assume each other's shape and garner each other's wisdom. By so doing, we come away with a different perspective. The illusionary barriers that separate us from the natural world fall away so that we are once again relating to the world in the way of our ancestors. Indeed, this spiritual partnership contributes to improving life and transforms your perceptions of yourself and the world in ways that enhance your creativity, too.

As with all other creative as well as shamanic tasks, merging begins with a strong intent and is followed by putting energy and action behind it, allowing the intent to actually manifest in the ordinary world. Shape-shifting happens on a continuum, from a very subtle merging of senses to a complete transformation into the animal or bird ally. While dancing along this gradient, a shaman is able to accomplish many different duties.

During the following exercise, allow your experience to unfold. Remember, this is all part of expanding your perceptions so that you can open up new avenues for your creative energy.

Merging with Your Power Animal

Refer to the exercise "Meeting Your Power Animal" for the list of what you will need to perform this exercise (see page 115).

Making the Journey

1. Get clear about your question, and write it down in your notebook.
2. Begin your journey in your special place in Middle World.
3. Call your power animal to you.
4. Upon meeting your animal, ask it: "Show me how I can merge with you for protection."
5. As you are taught how to do this, practice the process in the journey state.
6. After practicing, thank your power animal, and ask it what you can offer in return for this gift. (You can negotiate this until you are both happy with the exchange.)
7. Once you feel complete, thank your power animal again, unmerge again, and return to ordinary reality.
8. Upon your return, practice merging and unmerging in ordinary reality until you can feel the differences between being inside your power animal and not being merged.

9. When you are finished, offer gratitude to your power animal for its guidance and protection.

10. To fully return and allow your being to assimilate all of the experiences you had in your journey, eat your small snack and drink some water.

Once you become facile with merging, it's a skill that you can do at any time in ordinary reality. You can merge at times you feel that you could use a bit more protection or when you need an extra bit of vitality or strength to accomplish a task.

Process Questions

➥ What is it like to merge with your power animal?

➥ What did you learn from the experience? Write down all that you remember about it.

➥ Did your questions lead you to want to ask more questions on the subject? Write down those questions for future journeys.

➥ How did your perceptions of your power animal change after you merged?

➥ Under what circumstances in your life do you think that merging with your power animal might be especially useful?

➥ How do you think merging with your power animal might change your way of living?

WORKING WITH A HUMAN SPIRIT TEACHER: UPPER WORLD JOURNEY

Now that you have an understanding about asking questions and have developed a rapport with your power animal, it is a good time to do an Upper World journey to meet a human-form spirit teacher. The spiritual teachers found in the Upper World make themselves available to answer your questions, offer guidance, and encourage your own inherent inner wisdom. Like Lower World spirits, these teachers are safe sources of knowledge. These spirits, who have no need for a form, take a shape that is most useful for your interactions, which is most often humanlike in appearance.

Traditionally, the Upper World is a realm that is accessed by passing through the sky. In other words, you will be starting in the Middle World as you have done before, but this time you will travel upward. As a science junkie with an interest in space, I was put off when I first heard the inane idea of "passing through the sky" to get anywhere. I kept thinking about the levels of Earth's atmosphere, the solar system, the galaxy, and so forth. I resolved this mental sticking point by traveling upward inside a chimney! My intention for my first successful Upper World journey became: "I go to the Upper World through this chimney to ask my question."

Of course, if you aren't as stubborn as I was, you can lift off from a mountaintop or a similar high spot. Whatever you choose, you will travel upward until you encounter a distinct boundary that delineates the end of the Middle World. This boundary may present itself as a rubbery membrane, a ceiling of mist, a parchment-like surface, or some other sense of moving into another perceived space. Passing through that boundary you will find yourself in the Upper World. You will be calling on your power animal to assist you in this journey to meet an Upper World teacher to ask a question. As you did when you asked a question in the Lower World, always discern if the being you meet is the correct teacher by first asking: Are you my teacher?

Meeting a Teacher and Asking a Question

Refer to the exercise "Meeting Your Power Animal" for the list of what you will need to perform this exercise (see page 115).

Making the Journey

1. Get clear about your question, and write it down in your notebook.
2. Begin your journey in your special place in Middle World.
3. Call your power animal to you.
4. Greet it, and state your intent: "I want to go to the Upper World to

meet a teacher who can answer my question: [state your question]."

5. Travel upward with your power animal, and repeat your question at least three times as you make your way to the Upper World.

6. Once you pass through the boundary into the Upper World, look for a human-form teacher.

7. When you meet a spirit teacher, ask him or her: "Are you my teacher to answer my question?" If the teacher isn't the one to answer your question, ask to be taken to a teacher who can answer your question. Before you share your question, remember to ask the new spirit: "Are you my teacher for this journey?"

8. Once this teacher acknowledges his or her role in your journey, ask your question.

9. Once you have asked your question, allow the teacher to answer in his or her unique way. Your answer may be the entire content of the journey, particularly if your teacher replies in metaphor. Your teacher may speak directly to you. You may experience a journey within a journey. Whatever it is, just allow the process to unfold before you. If something doesn't seem to make sense, ask for clarification until you understand.

10. When you hear the drumming change to the callback signal, thank the spirits, retrace your steps, pass back through the boundary into Middle World, and return fully to your starting place.

11. When the callback is finished, take a deep breath, and gently remove your headphones and blindfold. Open your eyes.

12. As you nibble on your snack and drink your water, think about what you experienced.

As you continue to practice asking questions, keep records of what you realize about your own process. Practice going into a state of gratitude after receiving guidance. This is a concrete way to honor that which you have been given, and it strengthens your connections to the journey process.

If you didn't feel clear about the answer you received from the teacher, write down everything that you experienced to see if the answer will reveal itself. Sometimes clarity only happens in the writing.

This teacher can become a wonderful resource for you. Take the time to journey again to ask how you can step into an honoring relationship with her or him. Being in reverent participatory relationship with all beings—and especially with the spirits who teach, protect, and offer healing—is part of the ancient way of the shaman.

Process Questions

- ➤ What was it like to meet a spirit teacher?
- ➤ What did you learn from the experience? Write down all that you remember about it.
- ➤ Did your teacher's answer to your question lead you to want more information on the topic? If so, journey again to the teacher to ask your follow-up questions.

THE CEREMONY OF GRATITUDE

Since you have already gotten instruction earlier in this book about the usefulness of feeling gratitude, it is now time to strengthen that with a ceremony. Ceremonies are powerful ways to input information into the subconscious. As you perform a ceremony of gratitude for your power animal or teacher in the journey realms, you are teaching the subconscious part of your mind that this support you have received is *real*. In so doing, you are also teaching your subconscious that you are an expansive being and can travel to amazing places and meet extraordinary beings who are willing to support who you are and your creativity. Once your subconscious understands these ideas, they become an unshakable part of your being.

Performing a ceremony of gratitude can be very simple. First, it is important to choose a substance that you want to use for making an offering. Use something that is readily available and gentle on Earth and her creatures. Although it was common for the indigenous people of the Americas to use tobacco as an offering, in our times an overabundance of cigarette butts is polluting our world. Besides being unsightly, the tobacco in butts is toxic to amphibians and fish. While you may not live near a waterway, rainfall moving over and through the ground carries pollutants from the land, eventually depositing them into creeks, rivers, and finally the ocean, so it is best not to use tobacco. Asian shamans use many different kinds of offerings, including blessed water, milk, candy, flowers, fruits, and grains. The Native Americans of the American Southwest use a small pinch of corn pollen. Other potential offerings are cornmeal or another flour, dried flower petals, or birdseed. Choose an offering you can easily carry with you at all times. You may want to make a special pouch for your offering material so you have easy access to it during your daily routine.

Performing an Offering of Gratitude

For this exercise, you will need:

- A comfortable place to sit, lie down, or move safely
- Your sketch/notebook and a pen
- Your offering material
- A snack and water to drink after your ceremony

Making the Offering

1. Choose a place and time that make sense to you for your offering. Remember, this doesn't have to be complicated. You can set out an offering as you go out your front door each day, or feed the spirits just before you get into your car. You can step outside for a bit in the morning while your coffee perks.

2. It is imperative to enter into feeling gratitude before you make your offering. This emotional content is the fuel to shift your reality. The action of making an offering helps you to remember and produce the feeling. When you are in gratitude, you create a change in your subconscious as it pays attention to everything you think, do, and say.

3. When you feel completely full of gratitude, give thanks for your experiences with your power animal and teacher with a small offering from the heart. Take a pinch of whatever safe substance you have

chosen to use and place it on the land or into the water or up into the air with reverence. Consciously breathe in with gratitude and breathe it out again. Then go about your day.

This simple action can transform your baseline feelings about yourself and the world around you. You are reprogramming your subconscious to perceive the world as a much bigger and more glorious world than you ever did before and as a giving place. You are training your consciousness to recognize and acknowledge that you are living in a bountiful world and receiving things for which you can offer sincere thanks.

A small bag or pouch makes it much easier to take offering materials, such as flower petals or cornmeal, with you everywhere.

Process Questions

- ↠ What did you feel as you made your gratitude offering?
- ↠ How did your hearing, sight, touch, and sense of smell shift as you made your gratitude offering?
- ↠ How might you add this ceremony to your daily life?
- ↠ What are the times of day that you will choose to make a simple offering?
- ↠ Why do those times of day feel important to you?
- ↠ Think about how making these offerings could contribute to your experience of daily life.

As you continue making offerings, notice how your feelings and attitudes begin to shift. Make notes about these changes in your sketch/notebook.

JOURNEYING AND YOUR CREATIVE MUSE

By now, you have made a few journeys and have deepened connections with your power animal and a teacher. Take a moment to feel what has shifted in you. As you notice, breathe deeply and smile. You are progressively weaving an entirely new sense of reality while simultaneously unleashing more of your amazing creative mind. While the shifts to your brain take time, the more that you practice journeying with the drumming recording, the faster the changes will become hardwired.

One of the wonderful things about journeying is that you can use it to refresh your imagination and stimulate new creative thoughts. I have resolved stuck places while working on a painting and also in my writing. I asked to receive information that could support me to resolve the stuck place, and it always worked. The process of journeying actually strengthens the creative flow and helps the nonlinear mind to be more vigorous in delivering its gifts. Practice journeying often. It's the equivalent of traveling to your creative muse's door instead of waiting for her or him to call. Over time and with practice, you will experience your own sustained boost of creativity.

Since I've mentioned the creative muse, this might be a good time to meet a creative mentor using the journey process. Like your power animal and teacher-guide, a spiritual creative mentor can be a phenomenal support to your creative process.

A spiritual creative mentor might be the spirit of a renowned artist, inventor, writer, or musician from the past whom you admire. Just imagine receiving guidance from such creative minds of the past as artist-inventor Leonardo da Vinci; visionary architect Zaha Hadid; inventor Nikola Tesla; authors Charlotte, Anne, and Emily Brontë; theoretical physicist Stephen Hawking; painter Georgia O'Keeffe; Noble Prize–winning geneticist Barbara McClintock; poet, composer, and performer Leonard Cohen; writer, composer, philosopher, and founder of scientific natural history Hildegard von Bingen; inventor George de Mestral; visionary writer Octavia Butler; visionary architect, systems theorist, and futurist Buckminster Fuller; Noble Prize–winning author Toni Morrison; poet and fantasy writer J. R. R. Tolkien—or innumerable others. It might also be someone who was incredibly creative but whose name was lost to history.

What follows is an exercise to meet a creative mentor. If you have one in mind, make that a part of your intention, or you could ask for the creative mentor that is best for you. You may be delightfully surprised about whom it turns out to be.

Meeting Your Creative Mentor

Refer to the exercise "Meeting Your Power Animal" for the list of what you will need to perform this exercise (see page 115).

Making the Journey

1. Get clear about your question, and write it down in your notebook.
2. Begin your journey in your special place in the Middle World.
3. Call your power animal to you.

4. Greet it, and state your intent: "Take me to the Upper World to meet my creative mentor" (or if you'd like to meet someone specific, ask for that person).

5. Travel upward with your power animal, and repeat your question at least three times as you make your way up to the Upper World.

6. Once you pass through the boundary into the Upper World, look for a human-form teacher.

7. When you meet a spirit teacher, ask him or her: "Are you my creative mentor?" If that being isn't the one, ask again to be taken to your creative mentor.

8. Once you connect, get to know this new ally.

9. Your mentor may speak directly to you or connect to you through metaphor or symbols. Your mentor may also take you on a journey within a journey. Whatever it is, just allow the process to unfold before you. If something doesn't seem to make sense, ask for clarification until you understand.

10. When you hear the drumming change to the callback signal, thank the mentor, retrace your steps, pass back through the boundary into Middle World, and return completely to your starting place once again.

11. When the callback is finished, take a deep breath, and gently remove your headphones and blindfold. Open your eyes.

12. As you eat your snack and drink your water, honor yourself for being willing to meet a mentor to enhance your creativity.

Take time to internalize and process what you experienced. If you didn't meet a mentor, be persistent and journey again at a later time. Anything important in life deserves persistence and patience. If you get frustrated, keep practicing shifting into gratitude to move you out of those restrictive feelings.

Process Questions

➻ What was it like to meet a creative mentor?

➻ What did you learn from him or her? Record the information you received and how you received it.

➼ Do you feel differently about your own creativity after meeting a creative mentor?

➼ Did your first visit lead you to want to ask more questions of your mentor? Write them down as intentions for future journey meetings with your creative mentor.

As you continue to meet with your mentor and ask her or him questions, keep records of what you realize about your own process. Practice going into a state of gratitude after receiving guidance. This is a concrete way to honor that which you have been given, and it strengthens your connections to the journey process.

JOURNEYS TO THE ANCESTORS

Earlier in this book, I wrote about the importance of recalling your ancestors before tackling a task. You learned that people who did that were much more effective in their lives. Now that you have learned something about journeying, it would be useful to actually meet and work with ancestors who could support your creativity.

Most indigenous shamans cultivate relationships with their ancestors, and I have found having an ancestral guide has been invaluable. My primary journey teacher is my great-great-grandmother. Along with being a mother of seven and running a rooming house, she practiced the herbal medicine taught to her by her German mother. As with many of the matriarchs in my family, she was a strong and determined woman performing tasks that went beyond the usual scope of a woman's role. She also broke the usual boundaries that kept ethnic groups apart in late-nineteenth-century New York by treating people regardless of their ethnicity or religion.

I initially wanted to meet her to learn how to make her drawing salve (a skin ointment for drawing out foreign objects, such as a splinter, or pus from an abscess), as she left no records of her methods or the formulas she used. In my journeys, I was able to meet her, learn how to gather the necessary ingredients, and prepare her salve. It is the exact same salve I remember using when I was young, and it works the same, too. As an honoring to her for this gift, I make batches every few years and use them as gifts and offerings.

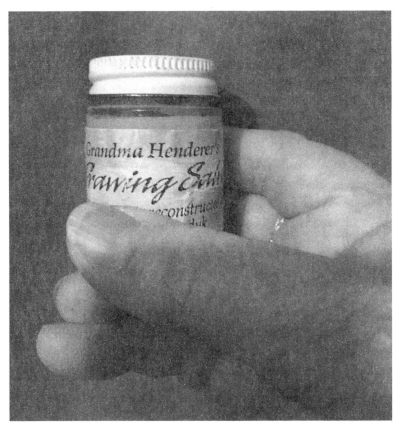

A jar from the first batch I made of my great-great-grandmother's drawing salve. It is over three decades old and still effective.

Over the course of my thirty-year relationship with my great-great-grandmother, she has become a trusted ally in my life and has helped many of my clients with her practical wisdom. I call on her to help with my personal conundrums and also as an emissary for the rest of my ancestors. She has introduced me to many of them, and all have been supportive in helping me to navigate life with more skill, grace, and peace.

In this journey you will meet an ancestor you may have already been honoring to ask her or him a question. Use your sketch/notebook to work out a good question to ask one of your ancestors. In this journey, you will be led to the right ancestor for your question, so spending time figuring out what you want to ask will help the journey to flow more smoothly. As before, read the instructions through before you embark.

Meeting an Ancestor and Asking a Question

Refer to the exercise "Meeting Your Power Animal" for the list of what you will need to perform this exercise (see page 115).

Making the Journey

1. Get clear about your question, and write it down in your notebook.
2. Begin your journey in your special place in the Middle World.
3. Call your power animal to you.
4. Greet it, and state your intent: "Take me to the Upper World to meet an ancestor of mine who can answer my question: [state your question]."
5. Travel upward with your power animal, and repeat your question at least three times as you make your way up to the Upper World.
6. Once you pass through the boundary into the Upper World, look for a human-form teacher.
7. When you meet a spirit teacher, ask him or her: "Are you my ancestor who can answer my question?" If that ancestor isn't the one, ask again to be taken to the ancestor who can answer your question.
8. Once you connect, get to know this new ally.
9. Your ancestor may speak directly to you or connect to you through metaphor or symbols. He or she may also communicate with you by taking you on a journey within a journey. Whatever it is, allow the process to unfold before you. If something doesn't seem to make sense, ask for clarification until you understand.
10. When you hear the drumming change to the callback signal, thank your

ancestor, retrace your steps, pass back through the boundary into Middle World, and return fully to your starting place and ordinary reality.

11. When the callback is finished, take a deep breath, and gently remove your headphones and blindfold. Open your eyes.

12. While drinking your water and eating your snack, thank the ancestors for the life you have.

Take time to internalize and process what you experienced. If you didn't meet an ancestor, be patient with yourself and keep on working with the process. If you get frustrated, keep practicing shifting into gratitude to move you out of those restrictive feelings.

Process Questions

- ➡ What was it like to meet your ancestor?
- ➡ What did you learn from him or her? Make a record of what you experienced.
- ➡ How do you think this meeting will change your way of living?
- ➡ How do you think meeting your ancestor will change your outlook on the ups and downs of life?
- ➡ Did your first visit leave you wanting to learn more? Make more journeys to meet other ancestors to learn more of their collective wisdom.

As you develop a relationship with your ancestors, you will also develop a more expanded idea about you. After all, the people who made you possible were creative problem solvers who are still very present in your cells. You are like a sacred bundle holding generations' worth of talents, wisdom, and brilliance, filled over the centuries by thousands of your people. While they may have had faults and weaknesses when they were alive, they are now a powerful engine of capability inside you.

If there is one thing you can be certain of, it is that your ancestors were creative. They may not have been painters, poets, or pursuers of some other culturally sanctioned creative activity, but they used their skills to solve the immense task of surviving and thriving in the world.

How do we know that? Just look in the mirror. They were able to pass on their genes down the long line that finally led to you.

Every one of us is here because of their efforts. They figured out how to make tools from stone. Later on, they smelted ore to make better ones from copper and then learned to make bronze and then iron. They learned to make garments from hide, held together with thread made from animal sinew, and later learned how to spin fibers from plants and wool and weave those fibers into cloth. They learned which plants were good for medicine and which for food. They also learned how to store that food without any refrigeration. The list of their creative accomplishments is staggering, not just the sheer amount of them but that each innovation was a first for its time. Every new idea was a creative leap of observation, exploration, experimentation, understanding, and implementation. Each one was an exercise of our collective ancestors' inherent creative genius.

While our creative ancestors may no longer be alive in their own bodies, they continue to exist in ours. In every one of our cells, we carry a sacred bundle of genetic material of the thousands of generations that preceded us. Not only are they alive in our bodies, their spirits are able to assist us with our daily lives.

A series of studies done in 2010, published in the *European Journal of Social Psychology,* compared those who thought about their genetic origins with those who made no preparation before taking a series of problem-solving and intelligence tests intended to measure how effective an individual is at meeting the challenges that may arise in everyday life.[6]

The results of the tests proved beyond any shadow of doubt that people who considered their ancestors before taking the tests received significantly higher scores. Reconnection with the ancestral energies imbued participants with better intellectual performance and enhanced their ability to find solutions. In other words, connecting with our forebears—even through memory and imagination—enhances our ability to accomplish the challenges of life with more ease and confidence. Interestingly, the tests provided the same results whether or not the test subjects knew or even liked their ancestors. In every situation, simply thinking about their ancestors provided the participants with a clear advantage.

It boggles the mind to realize that the generations of people we believed were long dead are able to assist us now, and yet it really shouldn't. Indigenous people honor ancestors as though they are alive. They are given special shrines or spirit houses in the family's home and are honored in some way every day, often with food. Along the way Western culture lost this valuable resource. This lack may be why many of us in the West feel dispirited or somehow incomplete. We are missing something vital, something that is both a part of us and part of what makes us who we are. I can think of no better time in history to step back into relationship with the ancestors and the remarkable resources they provide us. We need to be our best and brightest selves to tackle all that we have to do to right the ship and begin healing the damage we have done to Earth and her creatures.

By keeping our ancestors close at heart and in our minds, we are better able to solve all the emotional, mental, and physical puzzles that life presents to us with measurably more skill and grace. In other words, in thinking about our ancestors before we engage in any task, we unlock a storehouse of thousands of generations of talent to enhance our inherent abilities.

What follows is a simple ceremony to engage your genetic pool of creativity at any time.

Honoring the Ancestors

To perform this ceremony, you'll need:

- A quiet place to sit
- Your sketch/notebook and a pen

Performing the Ceremony

1. To begin the exercise, settle into your chair and close your eyes.
2. Allow yourself to imagine a radiant ancestral mother who has loving energy to share with you.

3. Meet her, and thank her for sharing her gifts with you.

4. Touch your heart with your open palm, and invite her to be with you.

5. Now imagine a radiant ancestral father who has loving energy to share with you.

6. Meet him, and thank him for sharing his gifts with you.

7. Touch your heart with your open palm, and invite him to be with you.

8. Ask your ancestral mother and father how you may honor them and all the others who have contributed to your being here.

9. Once you have gotten that information, thank them again.

10. Breathe deeply, and open your eyes.

11. Immediately write what feelings and ideas came from their presence. Then close your book and go forward with your day.

Continue to muse about your ancestors after this first meeting. As new thoughts about them or the ceremony arise, put them down in your sketch/ notebook in words or images.

Indigenous people make honoring the ancestors a part of everyday life in a way we in Western culture do not. Perhaps it is time we relearned how to be in relationship with our forebears, not only as a spiritual practice but also from the perspective of honoring their wise, loving support in our lives.

This exercise is one you can do before a challenging task, before you engage in a creative activity, or whenever you need a boost from the font of wisdom and power that lives in every one of your trillions of cells.

I have found that thinking about my ancestors each morning and thanking them in my morning ceremony have made a huge impact on my creativity, the quickness of my thinking, and the overall effectiveness of my everyday activities. It has also given me a deep sense of feeling surrounded by loving beings who have my best interest in their hearts. Like the early runners in a relay race, they are at the rail cheering their encouragement for me to live the best and fullest life I am capable of having. And because my deepest ancestors are also yours, I know that they want you to know that they're cheering you on, too.

Old photos of treasured family members and objects they owned
can be used to form an ancestor-honoring space in your home.

Process Questions

- How did it feel to think about your ancestors being alive in your body?
- Were you surprised to learn that thinking about them can improve how well you are able to perform tasks?
- What occurred inside and around you as you performed the ancestor-remembering ceremony?
- How do you believe working with your ancestors will transform your way of living?
- In what other ways could you honor your ancestors?
- How could you weave honoring your ancestors into your everyday life?

SIX

Shamanic Journeying into Unknown Territory

Now that you have had some practice with the Lower and Upper Worlds, it is time to begin journeying into more of the numinous world. This journeying, which is an extension of the journeying you have already practiced, will expand your perceptual map even further, expanding your mind's ability to more easily process new, unique information—a critical part of the learning process. Stretching the mind beyond its usual perceptual limitations also enhances the ability to visualize and pretest any new concepts or possible solutions to problems in your mind. In other words, you become much better at developing and refining new possibilities prior to actualizing them. This skill can save time and energy and also materials that would have otherwise been used to produce physical prototypes.

This was an invaluable ability for our long-ago ancestors. Imagine setting off for the unknown, entering a physical environment that is completely different from where you came from. All the animals and plants that you depended on for survival, food, and medicine are different. Our ancestors did that over and over again as they migrated and settled new regions on the planet. We began as dwellers of the savannahs and forests of Africa and moved into every imaginable ecosystem, from blazing deserts to the highest mountains and into arctic regions. Our resourceful ancestors had to rely on their imaginations, their ability to innovate new solutions and design tools to work with the new problems they faced. They accomplished all this without having a preconceived notion of what might be next.

Dr. David Kowalewski suggested in a 2004 article that "trackers in hunter-gatherer societies have an ability to extend their energy body beyond their physical body and see the creature's tracks somewhere else far away."[1] Ethnographers have observed indigenous trackers from the Amazon basin to the high arctic using such methods. In 1935, American ethnographer Frank G. Speck recorded a story of an old hunter in Labrador. The hunter had been tracking a bear whose pawprints suddenly ended; the rest of the bear's path had been swept away by the wind and blowing snow. There was no way to determine which direction the bear had taken from that point forward. Standing by the last clear pawprint, the old hunter squatted down and pulled a blanket over his head, plunging himself into complete darkness. He focused on the last print with his inner eye for a time until he began to "see" the bear's tracks heading in a certain direction. The old hunter got up and headed in the direction he "saw" and soon found the bear and killed it.[2]

The results of more than five decades of research into the effects the nonlocal mind can make on the physical world has made it clear that altered states of consciousness, during which the nonlocal mind is accessed and expanded, are real phenomena and have been and still are valuable for human survival and development.

These days we need to develop solutions for how to thrive in an environment that is changing around us. Whatever the challenges, I have found that taking shamanic journeys beyond what was familiar has better prepared me for a world that continues to change. I also believe these kinds of fantastic experiences have been contributing factors in supporting continual leaps forward in my creative energy by turbocharging my imagination.

Journeying is designed as a method for perceiving that which isn't as readily available in ordinary reality. For instance, journeying is a way to experience that which is too small, too large, too distant, or too faint to perceive with ordinary senses. When we stretch beyond the reality that is currently defined by our senses, we also expand our current construct of what is real. In some ways, it also boosts our sense of connection as we extend our internal map to encompass the nonordinary.

Once we have experienced a tree's sentience during a journey, we can no longer go back to seeing that tree as a thing or an it. The it has become a who. If we then expand that idea to our larger cosmos and to the past and future, we begin to perceive that we are integrated into a larger context; we are connected through multiple temporal and spatial pathways. We understand in a visceral way that we can never truly be alone. This feeling of being integrated into the infinite web of existence changes how we are able to be in our world. With such a perspective, we are more likely to be courageous about sharing our ideas and talents. We are more likely to extend ourselves by stepping into new adventures. We are also much more likely to be willing collaborators with others for achieving those things that serve our community and our environment.

These forays beyond the usual shamanic landscape encompass many different kinds of journeys. For instance, you might choose to experience a time in the distant past to witness something you have only read about. Or it might be exciting to voyage into a potential future that is not yet fixed or predetermined but based on current choices. Journeying to the farthest galaxy or into other dimensions of reality is also possible. Frankly, with the companionship of your power animal and teacher, you can "boldly go" where you have never gone before! For these "beyond the map" journeys, it is equally important to merge with your power animal. This will allow you to have deeper experiences while also knowing that you are both safe and able to more easily return to ordinary reality.

As if you had taken one of Alice's potions, you can grow very large or very small in journeys. You can safely dive deeply into the normally crushing depths of the ocean or fly far beyond the limit of the atmosphere with ease. All these experiences work to free you from limitations you didn't even realize you may have. In being stretched, you become more courageous, more expansive, and much more liberated in your out-of-the-box thinking.

As you journey into unknown territory, you may find that these experiences not only stretch your mind's perceptions but that they also teach your body that you are not limited by ordinary space-time. Your physical body holds memories that can limit your creativity. They might be memories of loss, failure, or some other restrictive belief. The new, extraordinary memories your body makes on these journeys have a way of displacing what no longer serves you. This is especially important as you age or if you have a physical challenge. To be able to experience true wonder and joy and to explore that which felt impossible is liberating. In that liberation, you unleash more of your vitality, which can easily translate into having more creative juice.

The journeys that follow will take you through a series of these off-the-map experiences. As you have done with other exercises in this book, take time to familiarize yourself with the directions before you embark, merge with your power animal, and *always* return at the call-back. The return to ordinary reality is where the real benefits of the journeys will be experienced. You will be able to be here now with more energy and vitality. You may find that the snack and water help you to ground yourself more fully.

As I've stated before, if you feel vague or ungrounded after any of the other journeys in this book, go outdoors and feel the breeze touching your face. Then focus on your feet, and allow yourself to feel that you are standing on the body of Mother Earth. Notice any trees, plants, animals, or birds that may be around you. Take deep full breaths, and feel the gift of being alive in this moment in space-time.

JOURNEYING INTO THE PAST

In this section, you'll be taking journeys into the past to have experiences that can inform your present. Whenever we undertake any journey, we can be transformed by the experience and by the information we receive. When we go into the past, we can learn from those who contributed to our being alive.

Cruising to the Primordial Sea

Refer to the exercise "Meeting Your Power Animal" for the list of what you will need to perform this exercise (see page 115).

Making the Journey

1. Get clear about your question, and write it down in your notebook.
2. Begin your journey in your special place in the Middle World.
3. Call your power animal to you.
4. Greet it, and state your intent: "Take me back to the primordial sea that incubated the first life on Earth."
5. Merge with your power animal, and allow it to guide you through time.
6. Once you arrive at the primordial sea, ask your power animal to show you the life-forms that flourished there.
7. Meet a life-form you are curious about. Get to know this new ally.
8. This being may communicate with you or you may connect through

The primordial sea is where all life began on our world.

metaphor or symbols. It may also communicate with you by taking you on a journey within a journey. Whatever happens, just allow the process to unfold before you. If something doesn't seem to make sense, ask for clarification until you understand.

9. When you hear the drumming change to the callback signal, thank the life-form, retrace your steps to pass back through the boundary into the Middle World, and return fully to your starting place and ordinary reality.

10. When the callback is finished, take a deep breath, and thank your power animal for this new experience. Open your eyes.

11. While drinking your water, think about how you and all life on Earth depend upon the waters of the world.

Take time to internalize and process what you experienced. Write down all of your thoughts and feelings about the experience this journey provided.

Process Questions

➥ What was it like to witness the earliest life-forms?

➥ What did you learn from observing them?

➥ How do you think that meeting them will change your way of living?

➥ How did your visit change how you perceive the little things you meet in your life?

➥ If your first visit left you wanting to learn more, make a list of potential questions you may want to ask in your sketch/notebook.

Additional Journey Experiences into the Past

• Journey to meet the first tiny mammal that is the ancestor of all mammals, including human beings.

• Journey to meet and thank humankind's mitochondrial mother.

• Journey to visit your ancestral landscape of ten thousand years ago.

• Journey to meet an ancestral spirit of a landscape feature near your home.

JOURNEYING INTO THE
VERY SMALL

Just as the past is normally hidden from our ordinary gaze, so too is the infinitely small. Science has created mechanisms to explore the extremely small, but these observations are very different from the first-person experiences you can have in the shamanic journey state. Like your journeys into the deep past, journeying into spaces that would normally be hidden from your senses is expansive to your creative mind. Perceiving patterns, colors, sounds, and sensations from the infinitesimal worlds can provide you with rich inspiration. You can also receive similar benefits from the shift of perspective. The very small has parallels to the infinite spaciousness of the cosmos.

Like me, you may remember the very first time you peered through the eyepiece of a microscope at a drop of pond water. What was ordinarily a mostly clear, empty-looking fluid bloomed into an aquatic landscape of amazing and alien-looking single-celled creatures. How marvelous it was to meet the slipper-shaped paramecium sweeping along with its cilia, easily passing the slower amoebas stretching and reaching their bodies along. You may have seen forests of rod-shaped algae, and if you were really lucky, you may have met the multicelled hydra. That half-inch-tall, tentacled predator is a minuscule relative of sea anemones and jellyfish and doesn't appear to age or die of old age.

Journeys into the very tiny can be as marvelous, awe inspiring, and wondrous as those childhood experiences. This wonder is important, as it is a necessary part of the creative process. When engaged in a creative task, you need to be able to wonder how something might be or how it could be changed and reshaped. You need to have stimulated your mind enough to be able to dream up new ideas and to conceive of what has never been. In the following exercise, you will travel into the tiny world of your own neural network.

Traveling into the Brain

Refer to the exercise "Meeting Your Power Animal" for the list of what you will need to perform this exercise (see page 115).

Making the Journey

1. Get clear about your question, and write it down in your notebook.
2. Begin your journey in your special place in the Middle World.
3. Call your power animal to you.
4. Greet it, and state your intent: "Take me into my brain to witness the electrical activity there."
5. Merge with your power animal, and allow it to guide you into your body and to your brain.
6. Once you arrive in your brain, ask your power animal to reveal the light show of electrical activity that occurs there.
7. With your senses, witness the patterns of electricity between neurons until the callback. You may also ask your nervous system what actions you can take to assist its function. Take time to receive your answers.
8. When you hear the drumming change to the callback signal, thank your marvelous nervous system and retrace your steps. Pass back through the boundary into the Middle World, and return fully to your starting place and ordinary reality.
9. When the callback is finished, take a deep breath, and thank your power animal for this new experience. Open your eyes.
10. Drink and eat with gratitude for the miracle of your nervous system, which allows you to savor the world.

Take time to internalize and process what you experienced. Write down all of your thoughts and feelings about the experience in your sketch/notebook.

Process Questions

- ❧ What was it like to witness your brain's electrical wiring?
- ❧ What do you feel you learned from observing it?

➡ How do you think this journey into your own body to experience its electrical nature has shifted your perspective?

➡ What other aspect of your physical body might you want to visit?

Additional Journey Experiences into the Infinitesimal

- Journey to the inside of one of your body's cells to witness how it functions.
- Journey to an atom in one of your fingertips.
- Journey to meet the beneficial organisms in the soil near your home to ask them what they need to be healthy.
- Journey both back in time and into the infinitesimal world to witness the moment of your conception.

JOURNEYING INTO THE VAST AND DISTANT

The late shamanic teacher Claude Poncelet supported his students to journey into the farthest reaches of the cosmos. It was his (and my) belief that gaining the perspective of what lies beyond our Earth gives one a deeper respect and love for our home world. To witness the smallness of our little planet, to perceive its fragility as well as its majesty, is something that can bring one to tears. These are both tears of sadness about how we have treated her and also tears of being gratefully overwhelmed with her ability to be a life-giving world in what is primarily an enormous sea of emptiness.

In addition, these journeys provide a much larger canvas onto which you can create your own life. It may be that contact with the infinite simply helps us to treasure the finite time we will be in these particular bodies with these particular personalities. It can stimulate our desire to be all of who we are and to do all that we can do, during our cosmically brief lives.

Since space and time are actually one thing, you will be journeying into the deep past in the following journey. As we learned from the Hubble Space Telescope's deep field image, the most distant galaxies are the youngest. If we travel far enough, we can meet the very first stars and how they organized into a galaxy.

Exploring the Earliest Galaxy

Refer to the exercise "Meeting Your Power Animal" for the list of what you will need to perform this exercise (see page 115).

Making the Journey

1. Get clear about your question, and write it down in your notebook.
2. Begin your journey in your special place in the Middle World.
3. Call your power animal to you.
4. Greet it, and state your intent: "Take me to experience the earliest galaxy."
5. Merge with your power animal, and allow it to guide you far out into the cosmos.
6. Once you arrive at your destination, observe and experience this early version of star formation.
7. With your senses, examine the stars there, and see if you perceive planetary bodies whirling around them. Observe and explore until the callback.
8. When you hear the drumming change to the callback signal, thank the ancient galaxy. Retrace your steps to pass back through the boundary into Middle World, and return fully to your starting place and ordinary reality.
9. When the callback is finished, take a deep breath, and thank your power animal for this new experience. Open your eyes.
10. Savor your water and snack, remembering that they and you are a part of the cosmos.

Take time to internalize and process what you experienced. As you have done before, write down all your thoughts and feelings about the experience in your sketch/notebook.

Process Questions

⤞ What was it like to experience an early prototype of a galaxy?

⤞ What did you learn from experiencing it? Also, make a record of how you perceived the experience. Was it visual, auditory, and kinesthetic or just an impression?

⤞ How do you think this journey far beyond our solar system will change your perceptions of reality?

Additional Journey Experiences into the Infinite

• Journey to the farthest quasar (the brightest and most distant objects in our cosmos) to witness the very beginning of the universe.

• Journey to witness the birth of the solar system.

• Journey to visit the planet Pluto.

JOURNEYING INTO A POSSIBLE FUTURE

The future depends on the myriad of choices we make in the present moment. Hence, you may think about the future—and indeed all time—as having infinite depth as well as infinite length. According to ancient wisdom, as well as cutting-edge physics, multiple possible futures exist simultaneously. They are like streams flowing one atop each other, and the choices we make determine which path we will find ourselves on. When you receive information from a preferred future, you need to do journeys to find out the steps you can continue to make in the present moment to put you on that path. These "path journeys" are ones that need to be done fairly often to continue opening up the future you have seen.

Contrarily, if you perceive a future that feels to be negative in any way, do journeys on what steps you can take in the present to develop a more beneficial future.

✎ Visiting the Future

Refer to the exercise "Meeting Your Power Animal" for the list of what you will need to perform this exercise (see page 115).

Making the Journey

1. Get clear about your question, and write it down in your notebook.
2. Begin your journey in your special place in the Middle World.
3. Call your power animal to you.
4. Greet it, and state your intent: "Take me into the future to learn [state what you wish to learn]."
5. Merge with your power animal, and allow it to guide you into the future.
6. Once you arrive at your destination, ask your power animal to guide you to a teacher who can provide what you need.
7. With your senses, receive the information and wisdom the teacher imparts.
8. Continue with the journey until the callback.
9. When you hear the drumming change to the callback signal, thank the future teacher. Retrace your steps, pass back through the boundary into the Middle World, and return fully to your starting place and ordinary reality.
10. When the callback is finished, take a deep breath, and thank your power animal for this new experience. Open your eyes.

Take time to internalize and process what you experienced. Write down all your thoughts and feelings about the experience.

Process Questions

- ➻ What was it like to learn something from a possible future?
- ➻ What else did you learn from this experience?
- ➻ How do you think that visiting possible futures will change your way of thinking about the things that you deal with today?

SEVEN

The Ebb and Flow of Creative Energy

Besides being a skilled mechanic, my father was an avid sportsman who really loved the outdoors. When he was a young man in the late 1930s, he trained with an elder woodsman who taught him the ways of the natural world and how to hunt in a sacred manner. Every year, Dad would make the journey to Upstate New York to a friend's land to participate in deer-hunting season. As a result of his early training, he was a diligent and cautious hunter who was deeply respectful of the animals. Never wanting to cause suffering, he learned to be patient so that he could bring down a deer with one carefully aimed shot. As a result of his care and persistence, we always had venison in our freezer, and through his actions, he passed along his understanding of the sanctity of nature to me.

We lived on an island, and Dad would fish at every opportunity. As his eldest daughter, I would often join him. Sometimes it would be a trip on his boat. Other times, it would be surf casting, and at other times we'd be dropping a line off the dock. He'd check the weather and that would help him make the decision on how we'd proceed. Of course, weather wasn't the only factor Dad would consider to determine when and where to toss a line. Just as farmers have to follow the seasonal and weather patterns to be successful, those wanting to harvest foods from the ocean need to understand a complex intersection of rhythms. Before every trip, my dad would always consult tide charts. Based on that information, he'd decide when and where our best shot at catching fish would be.

Our sun works in concert with our moon to create the ocean's tidal flow, and because of the moon's closeness to Earth, it has the stronger influence. Even though Earth holds the moon in her embrace, the moon's own gravity causes a bulge in Earth's waters. As our planet spins, we experience a bulge and a trough in the oceans that we call tides. From our position on land, high tide is when the water is deeper and therefore higher on the beach, and low tide is when the water recedes. These changes in ocean water levels happen twice a day in most places. Of course, that's not the end of the complexity. During a full moon and new moon, the ocean experiences *spring tides,* when both high and low tides are higher than usual. During the time just past the quarter and three-quarter moon phases, we have *neap tides,* when both high and low tides are more moderate than usual. Finally, three or four times a year when the sun, the moon, and Earth perfectly align, we have what are termed *seasonal high tides,* when the water rises extremely high.

Locally, tides are further influenced by several factors. Along with gravity of the sun and moon and the rotation of Earth, local tides are affected by the pattern of tides in the deep ocean, the varying depths of the ocean around the planet, and the shape of the coastline and nearshore depths. This makes tide tables essential for predicting the timing and oscillation of the sea at any particular point. Even with that, tide tables are only predictions, as the actual time and height of the tide is also affected by wind and atmospheric pressure.

Finally, we have *slack tides,* when there is almost no movement. Slack tides are like the pause between breaths, although they can last for hours. There is a high slack tide when the water is high and unchanging and also a low slack tide, when the water has receded, leaving the beach, rocks, and weeds high and dry.

About now, you must be wondering why I've devoted all these paragraphs in a book on creativity explaining the ocean and tides. *It's because all creative energy is tidal in nature!* Creative energy flows stronger and weaker at different times. When your creative tide is high, your mind is more likely to be flooded with fresh ideas and concepts. If you are engaged in a creative project, you also have more physical energy to work on it. It is a time that authors, artists, architects, poets, engineers, and other makers live for. It brings a childlike exhilaration and joy that is energizing—nearly to the point of mania. You feel fearless and brilliant. The work you are engaged in sparkles with vivacity, and you dance with it as one would with a lover. Indeed, it is the honeymoon period of creative energy. However, just as high tide peaks with slack water and is followed by the falling tide, so does creative energy fall.

Most everyone I know with a small boat has miscalculated the ocean's tides at least once in their lives. Since water depth over underwater obstacles is highly variable with tides and weather, even a small shift may strand your boat on a rock or sandbar. There you will sit until the tide turns and you're able to float off the impediment. If you aren't prepared for it, a temporary stranding can be devastating. However, good sailors bring fresh water, food, rain gear, and life preservers and other safety gear to literally "tide them over." In other words, they have what they need to nurture and sustain themselves while they are stuck.

A creative low slack tide period may go on for a day or two or as long as it needs to. No amount of pushing, fretting, or stewing will help. If you rail against the situation, you can make yourself miserable and be more prone to mentally beating yourself up. During such a low slack tide period, thoughts can emerge that suggest what you've been working on is crap and that no one will like it. Other negative storylines about your self-worth may rear their ugly little heads, too. These may include fears that that you have no talent, that you'll never be any good, and so on. That nonsense is just classic "low slack tide thinking"!

Something to remember during low slack tide periods is that even the most beautiful beach or cove can be really stinky when the water drains away. All the marine clay, seaweed, and other smelly detritus that was tucked under the water becomes open to the air. In other words, it's

Your creative low slack tide is a time to nurture yourself.

pretty common to have negative feelings come up during a creative low slack tide. Most times these are transitory and remedied with some creative, emotional, and mental sustenance. However, if the messages you hear inside are repetitive or punitive, it may be indicating an underlying belief about yourself that needs to get healed. In that case, use the low slack tide time to get some help with those perceptions, as healing them is something that will sustain you in a permanent way. In either case, whether the negative feelings are situational or in need of healing, don't let it spoil your joy of swimming in the creative energy ocean.

I believe that a creative low slack tide period is the perfect time for sustaining yourself. I use that time to observe nature, to look at visually stimulating imagery, to read a great book, or to putter around the studio and play with materials that are different from the project I'm working on. This intense focus on something other than my project is nourishing to me. It also engages my linear mind. This gives my subconscious a chance to mull over the bits and pieces it has gathered and to begin quietly synthesizing new ideas. When my subconscious begins bubbling new ideas to the surface, I know that the tide has begun to turn.

If I am on a deadline, I may also edit or refine something I have written, even if the feelings of flow aren't there. At those times, I rely on technique to carry me along to the finish. The technique I've honed over the years is like the preparations the sailor has made. It tides me over until creative energy lifts me again.

I have also recognized that certain seasons of the year are more conductive to my creativity. Like those seasonal high tides, my creative energy is particularly high as the world around me begins slipping into autumn. I'm not sure if it is all those years of being excited about the first days of school or simply a mammalian response urging me to get busy preparing for the coming winter, but I can feel a jolt of creativity energy surging forward with the first cool snap in the air. Since I know that is part of my personal creative tidal flow, I make preparations by filling myself up with ideas, images, and other nurturance in late summer.

Recognizing the feel of your own creative tidal rhythm can help you to be more productive when it is high and know how to care for yourself when it isn't. When creative energy ebbs, it can feel awful. The mind can begin to whir with worry, and you can feel the damp fog of a gloomy mood creeping in. However, when you learn more about your own unique creative tides, you can better recognize when the tide is receding and change your course to one of nurturance. That way, you'll be positioned to float up on the next incoming tide.

Charting Your Creative Tidal Flow

For this you'll need:

- A wall calendar with big day blocks to write in
- A set of kids' markers
- Some little stickers about a quarter of the size of the calendar's day blocks

As with other exercises, read through the directions before you begin.

1. For the next year, mark each high creative energy day with a high-energy, warm color of your choice. Also mark the days your creative energy is low with a suitably cooler, more subdued color.
2. Be sure to also choose a third color for marking the days you intentionally focus on your own nurturance.
3. As patterns emerge, you may also find that certain times of the day are more conductive to creative energy. If that happens, use your stickers to indicate peak times of day.
4. As you proceed, write thoughts about what you notice about your rhythms in your ever-present sketch/notebook.

Process Questions

➥ What did it feel like to think about your creativity as being tidal in nature?
➥ As you track your rhythms, notice the feelings, thoughts, and sensations that accompany each phase.
➥ Pay attention to any patterns you begin to notice.
➥ Keep track of any new realizations you have as the year progresses.

Attending to your overall creative energy can help nurture flow, and learning some strategies to cope with the next low slack tide will become part of your survival gear.

ENCOURAGING THE FLOW OF CREATIVE ENERGY

Opening up your creativity with the shamanic journeys and ceremonies in this book is only part of the process; being more creative also requires that you be willing to exercise daily your creative energy like a muscle. You may, however, struggle with doing the same methods every day (like me), causing you to feel stale or to become bored. Toward that end, I recommend a few different approaches and valuable practices that you can use to boost or sustain your innate creative energy. Give them all a try, as you never know what will encourage your flow.

DAILY CREATIVE CEREMONIES

The subconscious mind operates in concert with the conscious mind to create your life. You need to invite your subconscious mind to participate more actively in your life, to build a relationship with it and provide pathways for it to communicate with your conscious mind.

Many creatives devote twenty minutes each day, ideally first thing in the morning, to opening the spigot to their creative energy's wellspring. Some use that time for writing what Julia Cameron calls in her book *The Artist's Way* "morning pages." This free-writing exercise entails writing three pages of text in your sketch/notebook each morning. It is purely stream of consciousness and is done quickly without giving any thought to spelling, grammar, or punctuation. The writing is done in longhand to provide a direct and embodied connection with the page. Being unfiltered and free is the point of the exercise, as it begins to widen the portal to the nonlinear brain.

Another technique is to use the time immediately before you fall asleep at night or after you wake up in the morning to access images and thoughts from the subconscious. This transitional state of consciousness between wakefulness and sleep, known as *hypnagogia*, provides a playground where conscious awareness intertwines with potent lucid thinking and dream images. This natural, liminal time is a perfect opportunity to allow the ideas that are waiting at the surface to burble forth. When I first wake up, I allow myself to remain still. Sometimes I stare at the sky out of the window, other times at the ceiling. That not-quite-awake state can be incredibly fertile since the linear mind hasn't yet kicked into gear. I allow it to deliver its gifts and don't write anything down until the moment passes. Only then do I engage my linear mind to record it on paper. It is critical to make certain that you don't inadvertently engage your linear mind by thinking about the day to come before you have reaped the harvest of your subconscious; otherwise, you'll shut the process down. This does require some practice and mental discipline, but it is well worth the effort.

The Subconscious Mind:
Your Creative Co-conspirator

You can also program your subconscious before you go to sleep, asking it to provide creative solutions through dreams. The subconscious can be creative when you are sleeping, and that is why you have started work repatterning its beliefs. You have been clearing the way for it to do its most amazing work. The prolific inventor Thomas Edison never even napped without programming his sleep time. He is famously quoted as saying, "Never go to sleep without a request to your subconscious." As I stated earlier, your brain naturally flows through a series of brain states when falling asleep, from active beta, to relaxed alpha, and into theta before entering into the delta sleep wave. Once asleep, your subconscious mind is able to solve problems and be creative, especially when you are deeply in the delta wave state. It can accomplish this because the linear mind is completely off-line during that period.

In this way, your subconscious becomes what professor and neurobiologist Stuart Thompson describes as "your tireless co-conspirator."[1] It is also why I suggested clearing it of unbeneficial beliefs: that old clutter just takes up space that you want for your creative energy to flow.

As you did with your clearing process, take time before going to bed to think about what you want to accomplish or what problem you want to solve. Look at it from as many angles are you can and develop a request(s) about it for your subconscious mind. Keep your requests simply worded, and make them clear. Finally, write them down, and then get into bed. As you are falling into sleep, visualize and *feel* what it is you want the subconscious to work on as if it is already accomplished, and then use your voice to say, "I am grateful to my mind for providing me input about [insert request here]."

The ideas, concepts, and solutions the subconscious develops during this time can be harvested in the morning if you preserve the time your mind begins to wake up for that purpose. This means allowing yourself to linger in that hypnagogic state before the linear mind fully goes back online for your day. If I wake up in the night, I allow the nonlinear mind free rein again. If I get a wonderful idea at that time, I don't engage the linear mind with writing as it can keep me from returning to sleep. Instead, I ask my mind to remember it for the morning. Having practiced this for years, the idea that came to me in the night will surface again in my morning time. Make sure you use your sketch/notebook to capture the ideas that bubble forth when you are fully awake.

A wonderful step toward this is to begin intentionally shaping and recalling your dreams. I have already shared how giving messages to the subconscious during the time just before sleep, when your brain is producing theta waves, can be incredibly useful in altering internal limitations. This time period can also turn your dream time into creative time by using similar methods.

Shaping and Remembering Your Dreams

For this you will need your sketch/notebook to capture dream imagery that may have arisen while you were dreaming. Place that and a small flashlight directly next to your bed so that it is easily accessible in the night.

1. Create an intention that you want your dreams to address. This is called shaping your dreamscape. In essence, you are giving a problem to solve to the subconscious mind to play with while you are sleeping.
2. Write that intent on a fresh page in your sketch/notebook.
3. Climb into bed, and get comfortable.
4. Allow yourself to breathe deeply and restfully.
5. Repeat the intention you have written down as a quiet mantra until you fall asleep.
6. When you are aware you have had a dream, stay in the same position *with your eyes closed* and recall the dream in as much detail as you are able.

7. Summarize the dream in as few words as possible into your sketch/notebook, and go back to sleep.

8. In the morning, expound on your brief notes by writing down the dream in as much detail as you can remember.

Do this with all of your dreams and resultant felt experiences. *Keep track of all new realizations or changes of awareness you have as the year progresses.*

Process Questions

➤ What did it feel like to think about shaping your dreams?

➤ How many details of your dreams did you remember? How do you think you might remember even more?

➤ Pay attention to any patterns you begin to notice as you continue this process.

As you practice this, don't worry if other dream material arises, as this may be something your subconscious is asking your conscious mind to address. This is a fertile opportunity for the waking and subconscious minds to enter into a dialogue. If that happens, remember that given the opportunity, our dreams will lead us to and through the transformation of unwanted experiences. Our self longs for wholeness.

Also, if you awaken without a dream, just repeat the steps and go back to sleep. With practice this can be a powerful tool. Keep repeating this process until you have the answers you need.

To give you some encouragement, I'll share a little story of just how effective this process is in getting things done. Over twenty-five years ago, my partner and I were about to teach our first graduate-level training in advanced shamanism and shamanic healing. We had accumulated a great group of people who had already taken our apprenticeship program and wanted to study further. Using our own ideas, we put together a rough framework for the two-year-long program. Using the resource of shamanic journeying described, we expected to get clarity about what specific exercises would be best for each session.

No matter how much we tried, we were stonewalled. I finally asked the spirit of my great-great-grandmother, who is my primary tutelary resource, why this was happening. She told me this was to be a new "trust walk" in my process and that each session would be given to me in dreams just prior to the session. Needless to say, this freaked my partner and me out! We had a good group of people registered, and we certainly didn't want to disappoint them. However, I trusted this spirit implicitly, and so I bravely proceeded to the facility we had rented for the program with only the barest threads of a curriculum.

At night, I asked for what we were to do the next morning. Each day, I napped after lunch to get the details about the afternoon session and took another short nap after supper to receive the evening session's material. Believe it or not, the program was amazing. My creative subconscious mind worked in concert with the spiritual guidance I received to make a truly transformative program, but more important, I had learned to trust my own process to a much deeper degree. Nothing like a trial by fire to give you a sense of accomplishment. I had the incredible realization that my creative energy was connected to the ultimate creative energy of the cosmos and so was actually unlimited. It's also why I feel it is so important to stimulate your creativity. You have those same connections: no one is separate from the larger cosmos. You and I and everything we know were born from it and meant to express its creative energy.

BUSY BRAIN AS
A CREATIVE PLAYGROUND

Great ideas can also strike when you are fully involved in another task. The nonlinear creative mind steps forward when your linear mind is either so engaged it doesn't have any circuits left to suppress the nonlinear mind or too bored by whatever you're doing that it powers down a bit. Either situation can be fertile ground for sprouting ideas. When an idea strikes, stop what you are doing as soon as you are able and write down whatever arose from your creative mind. Even rough scraps of ideas must not be lost by being too busy. Think of your ideas like produce: they are best when you get them fresh.

Keep working with your sketch/notebook to capture ideas, concepts, and thoughts as they arise. Discipline yourself to carry it everywhere and use it often.

CEREMONIAL OPENINGS

Along with doing exercises such as writing morning pages and allowing the nonlinear mind to speak on either side of sleep, I find setting an intentional opening for my day to be equally important. While I liken it to having a daily road map, it isn't about choosing a fixed emotional, mental, or physical destination but instead using the time to choose a "road" that you want to travel. This is a variation on the mystery road trips I'd take with my paternal grandfather. He was great for taking a road he'd never driven on before just to see where it went. To this day, I like to follow this idea when making long drives. Without consulting any guidance from phone apps or GPS, I take an exit and go wandering. Using this method, I have stumbled on great restaurants with home-cooked food and curious roadside attractions and have had many memorable adventures.

Choosing a metaphoric path to travel each day can set a tone that is conducive to experiencing life in a vital, enhancing way. Now you could use this exercise for a specific project, but it is a lot more fun to use it to break out of your comfort zone and go off the map. Below are suggested off-the-map journeys.

- Choose to be open to signs from the universe for a day.
- Ask a stranger to tell you something that he or she always wanted to share.

- Use your camera to photograph only things or people with names that begin with a specific letter.
- Blow bubbles with the neighborhood kids.
- Spend the entire day without using *any* of your gadgets.
- Write "You are a miracle!" on fifty sticky notes and then surreptitiously post them all around your town without getting caught.
- Pack a picnic to have with a friend in the moonlight and choose foods that fit the occasion (moonpies, anyone?).
- Set up a mystery date with a friend that involves dressing in disguise.
- Decide to engage in something that gets you out of your comfort zone.

Use your evening subconscious programming to request what physically safe but comfort-zone-busting activity you can do the next day. Once you have heard from your subconscious in the morning, write it down before your party-pooper linear mind chimes in. After you've captured the idea on paper, follow through with what you received. Don't let yourself weasel out of rattling your own cage. As the ad says, *just do it!*

THE GRATEFUL HEART

As a part of setting my path every morning, I engage in a gratitude fest. I do this after I've sat with my post-sleep liminal state and written down in my sketch/notebook whatever fresh goodies my subconscious and nonlinear thoughts have delivered to me. I may even wait to do the fest until after I'm dressed and downstairs—as then I can step outside to do this ceremony. But I always refrain from thinking about the day's to-do list until after I've finished with my gratitude ceremony.

For my gratitude fest, I find it really important to speak aloud. That way, my subconscious as well as my conscious mind can hear me. I start with something like, "I feel grateful for this new day." Then I often follow with gratitude for my senses. Next might be gratitude for my health and that of my partner. As I go along, I offer gratitude for our cat, my ancestors (I name their names and specific traits I inherited from them), my family and friends (again using their names), and our clients and my students. How the gratitude flows is never exactly the same, as I allow it to be both heartfelt and spontaneous. However, I do make the ending exactly the same each day. When I've exhausted my gratitude, I always end with the phrase: "And thank you for the miracles I experience today!"

Just saying that phrase programs me to recognize and consciously honor every gift I receive each day. The gift might be a new bird at the feeder, a call from a friend I haven't heard from in a while, or an unexpected check arriving in the mail—but calling these gifts miracles unlocks a door in me that then provides the universe a way in to deliver new delights.

Morning Gratitude Bath Ceremony

For this you'll need:

- Your sketch/notebook and a pen
- A small bit of birdseed or cornmeal (if you are doing this outdoors)

Read through the instructions before performing the ceremony.

1. Close your eyes, and breathe a few times with a focus on your heart.
2. Remember a time in the past when you felt grateful.
3. Allow yourself to fill with feelings of gratitude again for that experience.
4. When you are truly feeling gratitude, offer thanks *aloud* for this day and its many possibilities.
5. Express out loud your gratitude for being alive.
6. Continue expressing your gratitude aloud for all that you are truly grateful for.
7. When you feel you've exhausted your reasons for being grateful, say: "And thank you for the miracles I experience today!"
8. If you are outdoors, leave a bit of birdseed or cornmeal as a concrete

offering to seal the ceremony and as a gift to the beings of nature around your home.

9. Take a few moments to write whatever came up during this process in your sketch/notebook.

10. Now go about your day!

Process Questions

➻ What did it feel like to take a gratitude bath?

➻ What occurred during the days that you started with gratitude?

➻ Pay attention to any patterns you begin to notice as you continue this process.

Practicing this can really change how you experience life and contribute to the generous flowing of your creativity. A grateful heart opens up your full capacities, and when you are running on full power, your creative energy can flow like a river after the snow melts.

ENGAGE STRANGERS

Stimulating your creative mind can mean dipping into counterintuitive resources. Of course, like everyone else, I prefer some things and experiences over others; however, I make a habit of checking out new things that may not be appealing at first glance. For me, that includes allowing myself to venture down unknown rabbit holes—researching a topic I know nothing about, learning something about an unfamiliar culture, or exploring a new town. One of my favorites is chatting with people who either do something or are from a place that I know nothing about. I have learned about the complexities of being a harbormaster, tasted homemade blood sausage from Colombia, discovered what it feels like to go from being a refugee to being a business owner, learned how a turban is wrapped, and a bunch of other wonderful things.

This kind of exploratory play is fun. I learned the truth of that when I was a small child. I was raised in a service station that my mechanic father ran. My mom did the books for the business and would paint the windows for holidays. The station building was attached to a taxi company office where my grandmother was a dispatcher and my grandfather was a driver. This building conglomerate was on a bustling corner with a busy bus stop. All manner of people from all sorts of economic and ethnic backgrounds came into the station. Some of these folks were customers, others were friends of my family, and some others just ducked in to get out of the rain to wait for the bus. Since I was the only child there, I was spoken kindly to in many different languages, as well as in English seasoned with different accents. Under the watchful eyes of my adult family members, I was given treats, regularly danced the tarantella with an Italian man who was a knife grinder (and who always provided me with a quarter), wore hand-knitted or crocheted clothing that some of the older women made for me, and had a bunch of really extraordinary opportunities to see and experience new things. Best of all, I learned the importance of how differences make the world a sweet and amazing place. All you need to do is ask someone a question, and the conversation can open up a new horizon!

UH, WHERE?

Experiencing or immersing yourself in different places is important for stimulating the creative flow. In fact, a counterintuitive environment can be incredibly stimulating. By that I mean an environment that is different from your discipline or purpose. When you place yourself in an altered context, you learn a lot about yourself, and when you choose to work in a different context from the majority of people in your business or craft, you are more able to make distinct and unique connections. The more dissonant the place seems to be, the more likely you will be able to integrate and cross-pollinate different ideas. By learning to integrate information and ideas from seemingly dissimilar fields, you will be more able to avoid dogmatic thinking and expectations. In addition, when you place your linear mind in a counterintuitive environment, the nonlinear mind can break through the "regularly scheduled broadcasts" of your ordinary consciousness with extraordinarily creative bulletins.

Albert Einstein is a prime example of the effectiveness of this method. When Einstein published four research articles that would change our ideas about space, time, and the nature of physical matter, he was working as a patent office clerk. The Swiss Patent Office was hardly a university physics lab, but in that bureaucratic environment, Einstein's mind took flight. We'll never know if he would have made the same brilliant leaps if he had been working in a physics lab. What I do know is that working or thinking in the same way as other people will typically cause you to think and perform as they do. We humans are social primates and so subconsciously tend to mirror the thoughts and actions of those around us. Of course, that's just the old linear mind helping to keep us inside the safe zone of experience. On the other hand, your spacious, nonlinear mind loves to have things shaken up a bit. Basically, you have to add some dissonance to your life to be able to more easily develop unique ideas.

An environment that supports getting the linear mind out of the way is a coffee shop. I recommend going there with your ever-present sketch/notebook and just let yourself daydream ideas. Believe it or not, it has been documented that the sounds of a busy coffee shop or café can enhance creativity.[2] In more technical terms, a moderate level of ambient noise—such as the kind you might find in a coffee shop, a busy train station, or in a murmuring crowd in a city—likely induces a processing disfluency or difficulty in the linear brain. In other words, it can't decipher meaning from the sounds and so chooses to go partially off-line. With the linear mind quieted, the nonlinear mind steps forward, and abstract thinking is activated. Consequently, creative thinking and performance are enhanced. The key here is that the ambient noise must be at a *moderate level*. If the sounds are too loud, they will distract and interfere with your creative processes.

Additionally, if the ambient noises are too soft, the linear brain will kick into overdrive in an attempt to decipher the sounds. Moderation is the key.*

On this theme, I've found being in places that are busy but where little or no English is spoken is especially stimulating to the creative mind. I learned this as a young girl of around seven years old. Back then, I had a treasured transistor radio with a single, wired earphone that I would listen to under the covers at night. After sunset, some of the local stations would go off the air. In their place, I was able to tune in to other faraway stations. One night, I happened upon a station from Quebec that was entirely French speaking. I listened to that station every night and dreamed about what they were saying and what the songs were about until I fell asleep. My mind created so many scenarios as I listened to the sounds pouring from the earphone that they flowed into my dreams. It was magical!

Other environments that produce this phenomenon are an airport in a foreign country or an ethnic market where you can sit down to sip coffee or have a light snack. The buzz of bustling people going about their lives—buying produce, ordering food, gathering with friends—is joyful and provides that moderate level of noise conductive to creative thinking. One of my favorite activities is visiting a nearby ethnic market where I am surrounded by good energy that is never distracting because I can't understand most of what is being said around me.

If you aren't blessed with lively ethnic communities in your town, try listening to foreign radio stations. I have an app on my phone† that allows me to play internet radio stations from around the world. You can also find similar websites that offer the same opportunities. These

---

*If you can't get away to or live in the countryside, try websites with good ambient recordings: https://mynoise.net/NoiseMachines/cafeRestaurantNoiseGenerator.php, http://rainyscope.com, https://hipstersound.com, or www.coffitivity.com. I also use a paid service called BrainFM, which offers a suite of sounds under the heading "Focus" that are very helpful for creative thinking.

†The application is TuneIn, which can also be accessed via https://tunein.com.

services offer an abundance of stations that offer music and talk shows in every language imaginable.

So when you're feeling stuck with an idea, another good strategy for your toolbox is to shift your environment. Go to the local coffee shop, ethnic market, museum, or library. Let the unfamiliar buzz of noise open up your creative faucet, and for heaven's sake, don't forget to take your sketch/notebook!

NATURE ALWAYS OFFERS NURTURE

One of the best all-around stimulants to creativity and also wellness support is to go out into nature. Throughout time, writers, artists, composers, and other creatives have found both solace and inspiration in nature. It is our original context for living. When we bring ourselves back into its embrace, we are benefited in so very many ways.

While it's great if you can get to a wilderness area or a national park, a little city park can also do the trick. I have found that being under an open sky can really clear the cobwebs. Find some green space, and let your mind wander as you watch the clouds roll by, listen to the birds, or just relish the quiet.

Some people favor natural places near the water. Alongside the ocean, the aroma of the salt water and all those negative ions filling the air seem to be especially restorative for the nervous system. Similar effects can be found near any moving water: a rushing river, a waterfall, or even a park fountain. For others, a peaceful pond or lake is restorative. Again, if you are in a city, take advantage of duck ponds, reservoirs, and other waterways open to the public. Even a busy metropolis often has tucked-away places that fit the bill.

Coniferous forests are brilliant places to be restored. Evergreens such as pines, hemlocks, firs, and spruces all fill the air with a variety of aerosol compounds. These not only smell great, they are also physically beneficial. Diana Beresford-Kroeger, a medical biochemist and botanist living in Canada, has proven that trees load the air with compounds that are antibiotic, anti-inflammatory, antiseptic, antiviral, and analgesic. These natural chemicals, which they produce to protect themselves from parasites and disease, have been found to support animal health, including that of humans. When you are around trees, you absorb these compounds into your body. Even a twenty-minute session of what the Japanese have termed *forest bathing* stimulates your body to increase the amount of natural killer cells in your bloodstream. Called NKs, these cells help protect you from viruses and even from tumor formations. In addition, being with trees lowers concentrations of cortisol, supports greater parasympathetic nerve activity, and lowers sympathetic nerve activity. These combined effects lower blood pressure, reduce stress, improve mood, increase the ability to focus (including for those with ADHD), accelerate recovery from illness or surgery, increase vitality, and improve the quality of sleep.

Conifer trees offer forest bathers a medicinal
bouquet of healing aromas.

Being in the presence of trees also helps to quiet the left brain or linear mind, enhancing your natural intuition and creativity. One study by David Strayer, a cognitive psychologist at the University of Utah, found that subjects who spent three days hiking and camping performed 50 percent better on creative problem-solving tasks than those who did not.[3] He proved that being in nature allows the prefrontal cortex to downshift and rest. This part of your brain is the command center, responsible for what are termed *executive functions.* These include planning, decision making, problem solving, and acting with long-term goals in mind. When overworked, the prefrontal cortex can cause you to lose sight of the big picture, and your thinking may become natteringly myopic and stressed—all of which shuts down your creative energy.

While you may not be able to regularly devote three days to being outside, you can support your creative mind to be refreshed and strengthened by regularly spending time with trees. What follows is a simple meditative way to get the most benefit in as little as twenty minutes. Since this is a shorter time, it is best if you do this process two or three times a week. If you are fortunate to have trees around your house, just spending time with your back against one and following the breathing aspect of the exercise will be supportive. As before, read all the instructions first so that you are prepared for the exercise.

For your very first forest-bathing session, set aside two to four hours for an excursion that is at least a half mile long. Keep in mind that this extended time frame involves several stops for becoming aware of your senses, moments of sitting still, and mindful immersion. After having this full treatment by the forest, you will actually find yourself wanting to incorporate regular twenty-minute or longer tree visits into your life. In addition, you may find that you need to step into the forest for longer periods.

Breathing with the Trees

To perform this exercise in a way you can more fully relax, it is important to prepare well.

- Choose a setting for your time with the trees. Environments rich with trees or those that are mixed between trees and meadows are especially useful, but any kind of natural setting with minimal human-built features is suitable. Don't let choosing a spot become burdensome. Use what is close to home and easy for you to access.
- Take precautions so that you will be able to remain restful and peaceful in the forest setting. Remember to use sun protection and insect repellent to avoid harmful bites; most important, leave your electronic gadgets at home. If you must carry a cell phone for safety, silence it before you step out the door.
- Wear comfortable clothing that is appropriate for the weather and the season.

Performing the Exercise

1. Quiet yourself before you step into the forest or closer to the trees.
2. Step into the forest, and take note of your surroundings with all of your body. Notice scents, colors, sounds, and textures. Pay attention to where your body is in space, feeling your feet firmly on the ground.
3. Gently hold a leaf or branch while it is still connected to a tree. Do this with extreme care, as if you were holding an infant's hand.
4. As you make this physical connection, notice how you are feeling; also notice how the leaf or needles feel in your hand.
5. Offer your feelings of gratitude to this living being. Thank it for providing oxygen, and return the favor by gently exhaling onto the leaf or needle surface. Feel your gratitude pouring out of your body with that breath.
6. Release your physical connection to the tree, and now tune in to your energetic one. Close your eyes, and allow yourself to perceive the tree's energy. Allow yourself to connect.
7. While your eyes are still closed, listen to the tree. Tune in to even the smallest sounds. If there is a slight breeze, you may hear the tree creak or branches move. Listen for birds and insect sounds. If it is a wet day, listen to the sounds of water falling on the tree and from the tree to the ground.

8. Reflect aloud what you are experiencing to share it with the forest. Speak directly to the trees, to the birds you may have heard, and to all that you have perceived.

9. When you feel complete, thank the forest again, and quietly return to your starting place. Take nothing back with you from the forest but your feelings for the experience.

Process Questions

•➤ What did it feel like to synchronize yourself with the tree?

•➤ What occurred inside and around you as you opened yourself up?

•➤ What do you imagine the tree's experience of your presence was?

•➤ How often do you want to repeat this ceremony?

•➤ How did your experience of trees change?

When you are back in your car or at home or the office, take time to write in your sketch/notebook about what you experienced. Repeat this as often as you can.

SWITCHING TASKS

When you're stuck or feeling a lack of creative energetic flow, stop and switch to another task for a while. To keep the creative juices flowing, it's best not to keep at your creative task, especially when a short break doing something else can help you to reboot. This allows your primary problem to solve to rest on the back burner for a while. I think the mindless "gotta-dos" in our life are best for this: you engage the linear mind with a simple task so the abstract, nonlinear mind can be heard. Doing dishes by hand, weeding, folding laundry, washing the car, mowing the lawn are all good examples of these tasks, and I'll bet you can think of a few more. We are more likely to daydream while doing these tasks, which provides an opportunity for the nonlinear mind to step forward.

A simple method to do this effectively is to use a timer. Select a length of time that you want to be engaged in a creative task and set the timer. When the timer goes off, set it for a period for a different task or a bit of daydreaming. When the timer goes off again, go back to your creative task. Play with the timing until you find a comfortable length of "switch break" to enhance and refresh your creative juices!

THE CHICAGO DOG

As a born New Yorker, I grew up having mustard and sauerkraut on a frankfurter. That was the way everyone in my family ate a hot dog, and I came to love it. As I grew up and traveled around, I eventually encountered the Chicago-style hot dog. I was completely astonished at the amount of contents added to a simple frank! The Chicago version contained yellow mustard, chopped white onions, bright-green sweet pickle relish, a dill pickle spear, tomato slices or wedges, mildly pickled hot peppers (known as sport peppers), and a dash of celery salt. It's a "tube steak" and a side salad—just barely contained on a bun!

I'm using this culinary extravaganza, though it may not be appealing to your taste buds, as an example of another way to kick-start creative energy—that is, to cram your brain full! The process starts with giving your brain so much input that it overflows and then doing something that is relaxing and also moves your body. A relaxing amble around town or on a favorite path is perfect. Finally, you take some time sitting with your sketch/notebook to capture what was stimulated.

This exercise is particularly stimulating for my creativity. It is something I have naturally done for years. I found that if I input information that covered a wide variety of topics that are scientific, literary, and artistic together, my mind really begins to whir. As a result, I've made a habit of going to my office and filling up my brain before I engage in my mundane to-dos. While I'm engaged in cleaning or running errands, my brain chews all the bits so that when I get back to my office, I'm raring to go with a creative project.

As with other exercises, read the instructions through before you engage in the exercise.

The Chicago Dog Method

For this you will need access to a bunch of reading material on different topics you are interested in, audios you have been meaning to listen to that are also diverse, and finally a *safe place* you can walk in a mindless, ambling way afterward. Give yourself a couple of hours for this exercise.

1. Gather your materials.
2. Read bits of several books and web articles on different topics or listen to a few podcasts you've saved.
3. Then listen to snippets of several radio programs or podcasts, also on different topics.
4. Now go out and let the subconscious ruminate while you're ambling around.
5. When you get back, take out your sketch/notebook and just start writing or doodling. See what has bubbled to the surface.

Finding a diversity of input that interests you is key. Use your own curiosity to gather a mix that tickles your fancy. Not only will you unleash more of your creativity, you will have a lot more to talk about with your friends.

Process Questions

- ➻ What did it feel like to stuff your mind full?
- ➻ What felt different about your walk?
- ➻ What occurred inside and around you when you began to work with your sketch/notebook?
- ➻ How often do you want to repeat this exercise?

DREAM MOUNTAINS, NOT MOLEHILLS

Another radical way to encourage your creative energy to flow is to set wildly ambitious goals. In fact, Dan Sullivan, founder and president of

The Strategic Coach, suggests that by making times ten your measuring stick—that is, you aim to achieve ten times more than usual—you can easily see how you can bypass what everyone else is doing. Indeed, if you are reaching for a solution ten times better than others, you will definitely achieve grand ideas.

This absurd-sounding idea works because a really big desire that transcends everything else is intrinsically motivating. By its very nature, a big goal seems difficult, implausible, or even impossible, which gives your motivation more juice. More important, it is best if the goal also has a deadline. This creates a sense of urgency that can force you to trust the crazy ideas the nonlinear mind and subconscious are delivering.

Marcus Aurelius was a Roman emperor from 161 to 180 CE and a Stoic philosopher. He was the last of the rulers traditionally known as the Five Good Emperors and the last emperor of Pax Romana, an age of relative peace and stability for the Roman Empire. He said two wonderful things about this concept.

His first quote is: "Because a thing seems difficult for you, do not think it impossible for anyone to accomplish." If you look around you, a great many things that the common wisdom of the culture thought were impossible have been achieved. Personally, it is just this fact that fuels my vision that by harnessing more of our populace's creativity we can save and renew our planet.

Marcus Aurelius also said, "The impediment to action advances action. What stands in the way becomes the way." So dream big, give yourself deadlines, and take action with your creativity. If you shoot for the moon, for a dream ten times greater than others, you will manifest more than you believe is possible.

One caveat is to ignore what others in your field are doing. Focus on your process, follow your curiosity, stoke your creative energy, and keep reaching for your absurdly marvelous goals. Something wonderful will come from it.

Practice all of the exercises in this chapter until you feel changes occurring. Don't worry if they don't seem to bear fruit in the beginning. Remember, you are reprogramming yourself into a much more creative person. Be persistent and gentle with yourself. Over time and through repeated practice, you will have success.

EIGHT

Building the Imagination

Albert Einstein once said about imagination, "I'm enough of an artist to draw freely on my imagination, which I think is more important than knowledge. Knowledge is limited. Imagination encircles the world."

Imagination is the ability to produce and simulate unique ideas, objects, and situations without any immediate input from the senses. It is the act of forming possibilities; as such, it is useful in making existing knowledge applicable to new situations and solving problems and is fundamental to the learning process in that it supports integrating our experiences. Imagination is a uniquely human ability to envision, feel, and sense that which does not (as yet) exist and so is critical to creativity. Being able to imagine something has allowed us to invent new possibilities. From the arts to technology and scientific pursuits, imagination is what gives us the ability not only to ask "what if?" but also to visualize with our mind, body, and senses the myriad of potential answers.

Empathy is also tied to the imagination as it allows us to feel what it is like to walk in someone else's shoes. According to psychologists Daniel Goleman and Paul Ekman, empathy may be broken down into three aspects.[1] *Cognitive empathy* is the ability to imagine what another person feels and might be thinking. *Emotional empathy* is being able to actually share the feelings of another, and this may lead to *compassionate empathy,* which is the desire to take action on behalf of another person.

Reactionary politicians and organizations of the political right often seek to shut down avenues that encourage imagination in children as well as in adults. Cutting funding for the arts and censorship, such as banning imaginative fantasy from libraries, are examples of this. A lack of empathy makes it easier to divide a populous into "us and them" and to shape that same populous so that it more easily conforms to an authoritarian, limited worldview. The 2019 study "The Relationship between Emotional Abilities and Right-Wing and Prejudiced Attitudes" expanded on previous research that revealed that cognitive abilities are negatively related to right-wing and prejudiced attitudes. Rigid thinking suppresses the imagination and tends to produce suspicion about any thing or person that is outside of the current worldview. This also correlates with reduced feelings of empathy.[2]

The freedom to think, create, and explore are fundamental human abilities that have made us who we are as a species and so need to be nurtured inside ourselves, as well as in the culture at large. After all, we can all learn, read, and study to increase our knowledge base, but real, undisputed brilliance is born from a capacity to imagine.

Now, perhaps more than any other time on our planet, imagining new solutions for healing our environment, for developing true social justice, and for finding a way to create lasting peace are needed. But for any of those possibilities to come to fruition, you and I need to be able to imagine that they are possible.

As a young child, you were a dynamic imagination machine. Later on, school exercised your rational, linear mind to the point that your imagination got penned in. Since imagination is a vital skill in creativity, it is important to open it up again with exercise. With some practice, your imagination will zoom around like a young dog let off its leash.

CURIOSITY STRETCHES THE IMAGINATION

One pathway to opening up your imagination flow is to train yourself to be naturally curious. Getting fully engaged in a new topic gives the whole mind (linear and nonlinear) an opportunity to fly in a new way.

My own curiosity has served me well over the years. Long ago, in the dark ages before the internet, I got all my reading material and did all my research in the library. After exhausting all the books on the topics I was interested in, I would venture to sections of the library where I'd never been. Giving myself permission to explore led me to learn important things on a broad range of topics, and I discovered that my curious mind acted like a detective in a mystery novel. One clue *always* led to another.

The mindset I developed from allowing my curiosity to lead me has contributed to my fearlessness in attempting solutions to just about any problem. For instance, my curiosity about mechanical devices (from taking things apart to see how they work) gave me an ability to imagine solutions to other physical world problems. Although I am not anyone's idea of a seamstress, I can craft a piece of clothing because I approach it as a three-dimensional problem that needs to be solved by using pieces of two-dimensional fabric. When I accidentally downloaded a Trojan virus onto my desktop while doing research for a project I had to finish that weekend, I didn't panic. I immediately thought, "I don't know how to fix this, but I'll bet someone else does." So I opened another web browser and started looking for solutions. Those took me into the fundamental programming matrix of my computer—which I admit was somewhat hair raising—but after few hours of browsing chat rooms and trying different solutions, I removed the dastardly malware.

I recommend delving into things that stretch your cognitive bandwidth and challenge your ordinary way of thinking. Drive off your usual cognitive highway, and step into the worlds of scientific material, different cultures, musical theory, or whatever seems divergent from your current interests. (Over the years, my selection of books on divergent topics has completely flummoxed Amazon algorithms. Score: Creative Mind 1, Giant Mainframe Array 0!)

Needless to say, curiosity rocks. The more you use your curious nature, the more like Alice in Wonderland you'll be: curiouser and curiouser.

EXERCISES FOR BUILDING UP YOUR IMAGINATION

Being imaginative is certainly a necessary component to unleashing the flow of your creative energy. You were born with the ability to be immensely imaginative, but over the years, that which was easy as a child may have waned.

Scientists who study human cognition—how we think and how our brain does what it does—believe that our ability to imagine, to come up with mental images and visualize possible scenarios, and to arrive at unique ideas is a result of having a strong neural network that is capable of coordinating activity across multiple regions of the brain. That means, like all brain tasks, imagination depends on a strong neural net, and neural pathways only become stronger through repeated use. To regain the imaginative capacity of your childhood, your imagination "muscles" need to be strengthened so that the flow of imaginative thinking is fluid and consistent. What follows is a series of exercises designed to build your imagination. Read the exercises all the way through first, and then get to it.

Creating a New Bread Crumb Trail

The following exercise involves getting your mind to exercise its ability to be more facile and quicker. The quickness aspect helps to prevent your linear mind from preediting your ideas. This exercise is a variation of a game my partner and I play when sleepiness starts to creep in while we're on a long car ride. After a round or two, we feel refreshed and are usually giggling. The idea of this exercise is to come up with as many words as you can based on the previous word. For instance, the word *street* might lead you to *graffiti,* which might lead you to *paint,* which might lead you to *brush,* which might lead you to *dentist,* and so on.

For this exercise you'll need:

- A timer
- Your sketch/notebook and a pen

Performing the Exercise

1. Set the timer for two minutes.
2. Choose just *one* of the following words and write a bread crumb trail of as many words as you can that follow, as in the above example.

> museum
>
> sidewalk
>
> shoe
>
> sandwich
>
> rake
>
> picture
>
> stoplight
>
> pool
>
> tangerine
>
> key ring
>
> button

3. When the timer rings, stop writing, and take a breath.
4. Write in your sketch/notebook any feelings or ideas that this exercise stimulated.

A few words about this exercise: making this fun is part of reengaging the playful way you may have exercised your imagination in childhood. Toward that end, it's fun to try this as a competitive game with friends. Give everybody paper and a pen, choose a word, and use the three-minute timer. When the timer goes off, see who came up with the longest bread crumb trail. You can even come up with silly prizes for the winner.

The next exercise is about using remembering as a tool for imagination. When we are remembering sensations or emotional feelings, we are straying from our linear mind. Memory is created and stored throughout the brain, but some regions of the cerebral cortex have been shown to be associated with specific types of memory. The frontal lobe is associated with both short- and long-term memory, and the temporal lobe is important for sensory memories. For instance, the temporal lobe is the aspect of the brain that can bring back a vivid memory stream that is associated to a particular smell. It is why a stranger's perfume or aftershave can bring back a flood of memories about a particular person in your past.

Imagining Senses

In this exercise, you will be imagining three sensory experiences. One will be a sound, the second will be a taste, and the third will be a scent.

This exercise has three parts, and each one is two minutes long. For this exercise, you'll need:

- A timer
- Your sketch/notebook and a pen

Part One

1. Set your timer for two minutes.
2. Close your eyes, and imagine a sound that you love to hear. Imagine it as richly as you are able. You may recall the setting in which you heard it first.
3. Notice how it makes you feel while you are imagining that sound.

Part Two

1. Set your timer for two minutes.
2. Close your eyes, and imagine the taste of your favorite food. Imagine it as richly as you are able. You may recall the setting in which you first tasted it.
3. Notice how it makes you feel while you are imagining that taste.

Part Three

1. Set your timer for two minutes.
2. Close your eyes, and imagine your favorite scent. Imagine it as richly as you are able. You may recall the setting in which you first smelled it.
3. Notice how it makes you feel while you are imagining that scent.
4. When the timer rings for this last time, take a breath and write how this exercise made you feel and anything else that came up during the exercise.

Notice how you are feeling now. I'd be willing to bet you imagined a lot more than just the sound, taste, or scent in each part of the exercise. Your mind may have even wandered about a bit. Notice where it wandered, and write that down, too. What ideas have bubbled up? Where does your mind want to wander next?

Question Reality, Man!

In this exercise you will walk or ride around your town with a final destination in mind, behaving like a roving reporter. You will use the journalist's tools of asking why, what, and how questions about everything. For instance, when you see a stop sign, you might ask yourself: "Why are stop signs octagonal? What would happen if they were hung up like a traffic light instead of being on the roadside? What if they were illuminated? What might make them better at stopping cars?" Allow yourself to ask these kinds of questions, and other more outrageous ones, about everything you encounter. You won't need your sketch/notebook until the exercise is finished.

The instructions are simple:

1. Leave your home or office with the intent to ask questions about everything you see or experience.
2. Ask questions until you get to your destination.

Take some time at your destination to write down thoughts, feelings, and ideas that came up during this exercise. You may find that once you start asking questions, you'll keep doing it, and that is one of the best ways to come up with new ideas.

Ten Ideas

This is a variation on *Choose Yourself* author James Altucher's "Idea Machine" practice. He recommends doing this kind of practice daily. You are starting up your old childhood idea factory. It's stiff to start and probably needs some grease. Like exercising an underused muscle, the key to this exercise is to push through the fatigue and any "but, I can't" thoughts to make it stronger.

For this exercise, you will need:

- A timer
- Your sketch/notebook and a pen

1. First, do one of the breathing exercises in chapter 3.
2. Now set your timer for thirty minutes.
3. Write down ten ideas for a talk you could give. Yes, ten. They don't have to be good or perfect; they can be crazy, off-the-wall ideas. The first few might be easy, but you need to keep going until you have ten. You don't need ten *good* ideas, just ten ideas. Write ideas that your linear, rational mind tells you are ridiculous or embarrassing or downright bad.
4. When the timer rings, take a deep breath.
5. Save every idea in your sketch/notebook, no matter how out there it might be. Ideas always beget new ideas. And, the more ideas you make yourself create, the more likely you'll easily produce ideas like a well-oiled machine.

Mixing It Up

The intent of this exercise is to support you to mix the body of knowledge from one area of expertise and apply it to another area. For instance, composition, colors, textures, and shapes are the elements that artists consider in their work. However, chefs now pay attention to these same details in preparing their dishes. That crossover has produced much more interesting ideas and expectations about how food is prepared.

To do this, it is important to begin exploring subjects that are unfamiliar or on the periphery of your usual radar screen. For example, if you usually read nonfiction, try fiction; if you only listen to jazz, try listening to opera. That way, you will build up a storehouse of alternative approaches at the ready to solve problems. You can also stimulate the imagination with visual imagery, such as spending time alone in nature, particularly in a place you haven't been before, or by looking at unusual craft or artwork. Viewing the work of contemporary pop surrealists, graffiti artists, cutting-edge product or furniture designers, and other edgy creativity is wonderful for challenging the eye as well as filling the mind with new perspectives and approaches.

For this exercise you'll need:

- Your sketch/notebook and a pen
- Two books from different fields, such as fiction and nonfiction, science and art

Here are the steps:

1. Open the first book to page 39.
2. Go to the fifth sentence, and write it down.
3. Open the second book to page 55.
4. Go to the fifth sentence, and write it down.
5. Now create a story that invents connections between the two.

Remember, no thinking about spelling, grammar, or any other structure as you do this. Let your mind be playful.

When you are through, think about how your ideas flowed. Try to decode how your creative mind approached the problem. As before, also record any feelings that came up during the process.

Lateral Thinking Puzzles

Sometimes the best approach to a creative problem is through the side door. While much of our thinking has been trained to be vertical, following a step-by-step progression that eventually leads to an answer, it is important for those wanting to boost their creativity to learn how to think *laterally*. That means rejecting what seems like the obvious answer for what seems unsolvable and looking for a solution by searching for a new perspective.

This kind of thinking involves several guiding principles.

- Assume nothing!
- Break the rules.
- Be open-minded.
- Look for clues that others might have missed.
- Try lots of possible ideas before you edit them down.
- Beware of the obvious solution.

Visual and written puzzles that involve lateral thinking to solve are often used to stimulate creativity.

A classic lateral thinking puzzle goes like this:

A man lives on the tenth floor of a building. Every morning he takes the elevator down to the lobby and leaves the building. In the evening, he gets into the elevator, and if there is someone else in the elevator or if it was raining that day, he goes back to his floor directly. Otherwise, he goes to the seventh floor and walks up three flights of stairs to his apartment. Can you explain why?

If you think vertically, the puzzle makes no sense. However, if you start thinking about possible scenarios that aren't fully explicit in the question, you can answer it.

The answer is that the man is very short. In the morning, he can reach the ground floor button with ease. When he returns, he can only reach the seventh-floor button. He can only go back to the tenth floor if there is someone else in the elevator to push the tenth-floor button, or if he has his umbrella with him to press it.

Now you see that the evidence was there to solve the puzzle, but a step-by-step approach wouldn't solve it, as the man's actions appear to be illogical. Only by looking for another way can a correct answer be found.

Here are a few lateral thinking puzzles for you to try. Write your answers down and don't peek at the answers on page 192 until you've given each one an honest try.

Puzzle 1. A man walked up to a woman and handed her a book. The woman behind the counter said to the man, "That will be four dollars." He paid the woman and then left without the book. She saw him leave without it and said nothing. Why?

Puzzle 2. Little Billy was four years old, and both of his parents were dead. His guardian put him on a train to send him to a new home in the country. Billy wasn't able to read or write or remember where he was going, so his guardian secured a label on a sturdy string around his neck clearly indicating Billy's name and his destination. Despite the kindness and best efforts of the rail staff, Billy never arrived at his new home. Why?

Puzzle 3. A man walks into a bar and asks the barman for a glass of water. The barman pulls out a gun and points it at the man. The man says, "Thank you" and walks out. What just happened?

Puzzle 4. A blind beggar had a brother who died. What relation was the blind beggar to the brother who died?

Puzzle 5. A man was pushing his car. He stopped when he reached a hotel. At that point, he realized he was bankrupt. Why?

Puzzle 6. Bob entered a small room. The door closed, and when it opened again, he was in a large room. How is that possible?

Puzzle 7. A man dressed all in black, wearing a black ski mask, stands at a crossroads in a totally black-painted town. All of the streetlights in town are broken. There is no moon. A black-painted car without headlights *drives straight toward him but turns in time and doesn't hit him. Why?*

Puzzle 8. *Joey wants to go home, but he can't go home because the man in the mask is waiting for him. What's happening?*

Puzzle 9. *Quick, name an ancient invention that is still in use in most parts of the world today that allows people to see through walls.*

Puzzle 10. *Without lifting your pencil or crossing over any of your lines, draw the envelope below:*

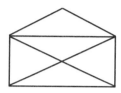

After you completed these puzzles, make some notes about your process, what thoughts came to you as you practiced, and how it felt to think differently. Lateral thinking might feel hard at first, but practice makes it much easier. That is exactly why it is useful to practice this kind of cognition. This exercise gets your mind working in a more expansive, out-of-the-box way. Learning, imagining, and finding new ways of thinking are vital for creativity and great for keeping your mind supple. If you're a mystery novel fan, you might be able to see similarities with how the detective finds the vital evidence that others have missed. It is a matter of shifting perspective, not settling on the face value of any information, looking for different ways to interpret meaning from the information that you have, and imagining many different scenarios on the path to coming up with a unique solution. It's elementary, my dear.

Process Questions

- ➼ How did it feel to do the imagination-building exercises?
- ➼ What occurred inside and around you as you worked with all the different possibilities? Was one exercise more potent than another?
- ➼ How did it feel to do the exercise "Ten ideas"?
- ➼ At what times do you think you may want to use these methods in your daily life?

Puzzle Answers

1. The book was an overdue library book, and the woman was the librarian.
2. Little Billy was a goat who ate his label, so the rail staff had no idea where he was supposed to go.
3. The man who walked into the bar had hiccups, so the bartender pulled out a gun to scare him. The man thanked him because it worked to stop his hiccups.
4. The beggar was the dead man's sister.
5. The man was playing Monopoly.
6. The small room is an elevator.
7. It was daytime.
8. Joey is on third base in the baseball game. The catcher is waiting at home plate with the ball.
9. A window.
10.

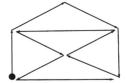

BRAINSTORMING

As reported in *Scientific American*'s blog, Dean Keith Simonton theorizes that those whom society deems to be creative geniuses depend on a similar process that begins with an "unrestrained search for ideas without foresight into their utility."[3] In other words, generating ideas for their own sake. Of course, this leads to dead ends, but then the creative mind goes through a process of trial and error, which ultimately results in a solution. In fact, mental wandering, process misfires, or detours may ultimately be necessary for innovating new possibilities. Creativity thrives in an unfiltered world that is unconstrained by preconceived notions. When we find ways to circumvent the rational mind's usual mental schemas, we break through to a new mental landscape of infinite possibilities.

Bamboozling the linear processes of the rational mind with alternatives and possibilities, no matter how absurd, is a vital skill for a creative mind. It is also at the heart of brainstorming, a term originally coined by an advertising executive. Brainstorming is the practice of generating ideas without allowing yourself to filter them because they aren't practical or useful. This approach encourages fresh thinking. A television show called *Whose Line Is It Anyway?* has a segment in which the assembled players invent unexpected uses for odd objects. If you can, watch a few episodes online or on YouTube to witness creative brainstorming in a humor context. It is a brilliant way to understand how, in brainstorming, anything goes.

Brainstorming combines a relaxed, informal approach to problem solving with lateral thinking. By that I mean looking at things in novel ways. It is turning a problem, idea, or concept around so that you are looking at it from a different vantage point. This approach encourages people to come up with thoughts and ideas that can seem a little off the wall. However, when the mind is unleashed, more often than not some of the ideas produced can be crafted into original, creative solutions or spark even more ideas. Because brainstorming is not the mind's usual, predictable way of thinking, it stimulates the nonlinear mind to make spontaneous leaps of creativity. In other words, brainstorming is a process that supports *divergent thinking*, the ability to generate multiple possible answers from multiple perspectives. During brainstorming, ideas are not judged as either "wrong" or "right." It's the process of coming up with *all* the ideas that are possible without judgment. When I was in advertising, it wasn't until well after the brainstorming process was complete that the process of *convergent thinking* was allowed, when all the threads were examined to decide what approach would be most desirable for the situation.

During brainstorming sessions, it is important to neither criticize nor praise specific ideas but to allow them to flow. Judgment and analysis shut off the creativity spigot and should therefore be reserved for an idea's implementation, not its generation. I have experienced some truly inspired brainstorming sessions that arrived at a unique and brilliant solution to a problem but were so open and fluid it wasn't possible to pinpoint who of the assembled group had first come up with the idea.

While typically brainstorming is done by a group, I have used it successfully to open up my creative energy when I have felt its flow become sluggish or while I'm on a tight deadline. Since you are likely an individual reading this book and not a group, I've fiddled with the process a bit so that you can brainstorm on your own. You can start by asking yourself some questions about a problem or project at hand. The idea is to generate as many ideas as possible—no matter how wacky they might be!

Read through all the instructions, and gather your materials before you do the exercises.

✍ Brainstorming for One

For this exercise you'll need:

- Your sketch/notebook
- A package of blank index cards
- A felt-tip pen
- A timer
- A stubborn question or creative issue you are trying to solve in mind

1. Open the cards.
2. Set the timer for sixty seconds.
3. On each card, quickly write a possible solution to a problem's or project's stuck point. *No criticism is allowed in this phase!*
4. Keep writing ideas until the timer goes off (shoot for at least twenty ideas).
5. When the timer goes off, take a big breath. There is a good chance that you're laughing at how fun it was to toss out ideas with no concern about whether they made sense.

6. Review the ideas, and pull out the ones that seem most interesting.

7. Use your notebook to play with those ideas, combining or improving them by asking what-if questions. Allow some of these questions to be crazy, too. Be playful. Ask things such as: What if this problem came up one hundred years ago? What if *The Avengers* were trying to solve this? What if [add magical possibility here]?

8. If the process becomes burdensome, stop and do something else for a while, but keep all the material you wrote in your sketch/notebook, including the most promising index cards. I always do this, as sometimes a too-crazy idea for one problem is exactly what is needed for another.

What Is It?

The same exercise as above can be done with an object or random photo. I've given you a stock image here to help you out.

In the same way that you did in the previous exercise, set the timer, and write as many wild and exaggerated uses for or origins of the object in the photo. Shoot for twenty ideas, and don't give up until the timer rings. Remember not to edit your thoughts, but instead just be as imaginative as you're able. Be as spontaneous and playful as you can. Remember, don't waste any of your sixty seconds on critiquing yourself or your ideas.

When you're done with the unrecognizable object, do the same process

This mysterious "what is it" photo is ripe for interpretation.

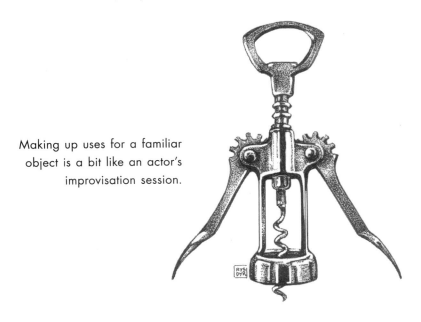

Making up uses for a familiar object is a bit like an actor's improvisation session.

for an object you *do* recognize. You probably have the object pictured above in a drawer at home. Ignore its original purpose, and go for just as many crazy ideas about what it could be or could be used for as you did for the unrecognizable object.

Once you've done these exercises, make notes in your sketch/notebook about your process. Make sure to include how you felt as well as what you thought during the exercise.

If you noticed that working with the recognizable object was a little harder, it is because your linear mind kept trying to get you to stick with the object's intended purpose, the only purpose the linear mind knows and understands. The faster you are able to ignore the obvious, the easier the process becomes. Try this brainstorming game with another photo or with another familiar household item. Better yet, try this as a party game with a group of friends.

A Three-Minute Story

Since you've been exercising your creative brain, try creating a three-minute narrative about who the people in the photo are and what they are talking about using the same method. Answer questions such as: Who are they? Where are they? What are they talking about? Give the most diverse, unique, and even absurd answers that you can muster.

These two people have a story, but only you know it.

For this you'll need:

- A timer
- Your sketch/notebook and a pen
- The photo of the couple

1. Open the sketch/notebook to a new page.
2. Set the timer for three minutes.
3. Begin to free-write a wild story about what's going on in the photo. *No criticism is allowed in this phase!*
4. Keep writing your narrative until the timer goes off.
5. When the timer goes off, take a big breath. There is a good chance you're laughing at how fun it was to toss out ideas with no concern about whether they made sense!
6. Use your notebook to play with the story, combining or improving it by asking what-if questions. Allow some of these questions to be crazy, too. Be playful. Ask such things as: What was in his drink? What will they do when they leave the café? Who is watching them with the camera? What if [add magical possibility here]?
7. Review the story, and see where and how it could be expanded.
8. If the process becomes burdensome, stop and do something else for a while, but keep all the material you wrote in your sketch/notebook. Sometimes what was a crazy idea in one situation is exactly what is needed for another.
9. Remember to make notes in your sketch/notebook about your process, and include how you felt and what you thought during the exercise.

The brainstorming exercise that I've just shared can help you to open up your creative mind. Take time to notice how it felt giving yourself permission for your ideas to be let loose. Don't worry if your mind is telling you that all of your answers were silly. That is exactly the point. Playing and experimentation is what creative thinking is all about. Baffling the linear mind with "silly thoughts" helps to loosen up your nonlinear, creative energy.

Keep the ideas in your notebook and start looking for and collecting photos that make you curious or are puzzling so that you can practice this exercise at another time. Images are easily found on the internet, in newspapers, or in magazines. Stash them in your sketch/notebook for just the right moment when you need a dose of creativity play.

Until you find some of your own, here are a few sample photos with idea prompts for you to make up new stories.

You've been walking down a deserted tile-walled hallway for twenty minutes. Just as you arrive at this old pay phone, it rings. Startled, you pick up the receiver and . . .

The barn behind the roadside café was a great place to stretch my legs. I thought I was alone when I heard a softly vibrating whisper of a voice say . . .

Jenny put down her metal detector. "Probably another old soda can,"
she mumbled to herself as she started to brush away the sand.
Then she saw it sparkle. "Whoa, a watch and it looks like gold!"
She lifted the watch up and turned it over in her hand.
Then she spotted the very unusual inscription on the back . . .

Process Questions

↦ How did it feel to do the brainstorming exercises?

↦ What occurred inside and around you as performed each one? Was one exercise more potent than another?

↦ How did it feel to write a three-minute story?

↦ What other ways do you think you might do brainstorming?

NINE

Embracing Your Highest Consciousness

Physicist and philosopher James B. Glattfelder wrote that "the human mind faces its own nature. By extending the information-theoretic paradigm, the informational nature of consciousness is uncovered. . . . The nature of consciousness, as has been suggested by ancient Eastern and shamanic traditions, is necessarily universal and primal. . . . The well-served and previously glorious materialistic and reductionistic scientific worldview is yielding to a novel scientific conception of subjective consciousness and objective reality—and their unexpected intimate kinship."[1] In other words, consciousness is the most fundamental essence of existence out of which comes the experience of material reality.

This idea is what I wrote about earlier in this book. Glattfelder is suggesting that consciousness, in its highest manifestation, creates and colors the fabric of reality. Ervin Laszlo proposed the idea of a *virtual energy field* that is pregnant with all possibilities but appears to be a void.[2] This quantum plenum has been described by theoretical physicist Mark Comings in this way:

> The word plenum means an absolute fullness and that's what we've got with the quantum plenum. It appears that the fundamental nature of so-called empty space is enormously energetic. . . . By many

estimations, there abides in one cubic centimeter of empty space an amount of energy greater than the total amount of energy contained or expressed in all of the matter in the known universe.[3]

The quantum plenum is a nonphysical field that is the ultimate source of all that temporarily arises into form. It is the energetic potential that is shaped by consciousness.

In relation to our creativity, we need to become more fully aware that our potential is actually boundless in its capacities. If consciousness or mind is paramount, as the latest thinking in physics suggests, we must begin to practice a deep creativity that is encouraged by experiences of expanded consciousness or awareness. In other words, we need to step into our birthright as creators. While this might seem the height of blasphemy by the dogmatic conventions of religious thought, it is not. If we are, as so many of our spiritual texts suggest, created in the image of the divine, it is necessary to refine our consciousness so that we (as members of our human collective) do not keep creating chaos in the world.

Toward that end, I propose an extraordinary journey, which I embark on as often as I am able. It is a journey of perception that requires a strong intent, feelings of deep gratitude, and a fervent imagination to perform. I believe that it is one way to elevate our individual consciousness and so contribute to transforming our collective reality. And isn't that what the most magnificent expressions of creative energy have always done? Great art was meant to irrevocably alter our viewpoint—music to open the deepest place in our hearts, poetry to teach us the extraordinary preciousness of the everyday miracles around us. As we expand into the highest consciousness, we see the world with different eyes; we feel the connections between all beings and find ourselves treasuring the smallest, most fragile aspects of our existence. In that way, our highest consciousness becomes a creative energy that radiates with a frequency akin to love.

The following exercise is a journey to experience the field of vibrations that is continually creating our reality. It is very important to read the instructions through so that you can memorize what you are meant to do.

Note: Entering into this exercise with your power animal while truly feeling gratitude is an essential aspect of the journey. The Radiant Field of Infinite Vibrations is continually re-creating our reality. By entering with a heart full of loving gratitude, you are programming that field to produce harmonious creations not just for you but for all beings.

The Radiant Field of Infinite Vibrations

For this exercise, you will need:

- A comfortable place to sit, lie down, or move safely
- Your sketch/notebook and a pen
- A blindfold or bandanna for covering your eyes
- A way to listen to your shamanic journey rhythm recording
- A snack to eat and a glass of water to drink when you return

Making the Journey

You may begin this exercise by standing or moving to help you feel more inspirited prior to journeying; however, once you feel inspirited by the movements, *lie down to perform this journey.* Please refer, as necessary, to the exercise instructions for "Meeting Your Power Animal" on page 113 in chapter 5 for getting into a trance state and journeying to other worlds.

1. Once you have danced, rattled, or drummed, lie down.
2. Put on your blindfold, and start the journey recording.
3. Begin your journey in your special place in the Middle World.
4. Call your power animal to you.
5. Offer your gratitude to this being who has chosen you.
6. Merge with your power animal.
7. Now, offer your gratitude to all the ancestors who have made your life possible. Especially remember each of them that you have known.

8. The Radiant Field of Infinite Vibrations holds all the people, places, and animals whom you have ever loved and all the experiences in your life that you treasure. Honor them all.

9. Now, state your intent to your power animal: "Give me an experience of the Radiant Field of Infinite Vibrations that continually creates and re-creates matter."

10. Since the Radiant Field of Infinite Vibrations is everywhere, all the time, close your eyes in your journey, and tune in to the subtle vibrations that are touching the right side of your body. Be patient until you perceive the sensations.

11. Once you begin to perceive the subtle vibrations, imagine that there is an infinite, vibrating space stretching beyond your body.

12. Now focus on the vibrations at the edge of the front of your body.

13. Tune in to the subtle vibrations that are touching the front of your body, and remember to be patient until you are able to perceive the sensations.

14. Once you can perceive them, imagine the infinite, vibrating space that stretches beyond the front of your body.

15. Now tune in to the subtle vibrations that are touching the left side of your body.

16. As you begin to notice those vibrations, imagine the infinite, vibrating space that stretches beyond the left side of your body

17. Now, notice that you are being upheld by subtle vibrations just beneath your body. Again, be patient until you perceive the sensations.

18. Imagine that beneath you is infinite space, which is vibrating and holding you up as though you were suspended in the middle of a column of water.

19. Allow yourself to be held by the Radiant Field of Infinite Vibrations that made you and every being and thing you love.

20. Place the following intention into this field of ultimate creativity: "Elevate my consciousness so that I may fully experience my role in creating positive change."

21. When you hear the drumming change to the callback signal, thank the Radiant Field of Infinite Vibrations, open your eyes in your journey, and have your power animal bring you back to your special place in the Middle World.
22. Return fully to your starting place and ordinary reality.
23. When the callback is finished, take a deep breath, and thank your power animal for this new experience. Open your eyes in ordinary reality.
24. While still feeling grateful, eat your snack and have a glass of water to settle the experience into your body.
25. If you still feel vague or ungrounded after your snack, go outdoors and feel the breeze touching your face. Then focus on your feet, and really feel that you are standing on the body of Mother Earth. Tap your feet to feel that connection more keenly. Notice any trees, plants, animals, or birds that may be around you. Take deep full breaths, and feel the gift of being alive in this moment in space-time.

I recommend that you do this journey often. Make sure to always enter in gratitude, as that puts you in alignment with this ultimate creative energy. Entering the field in gratitude has profound effects on our physical reality. I believe this strongly, as I have experienced it in my own life.

It is important to let go of expectations about what you may experience, as expectations can actually limit what can occur. No matter how rich our imagination may be, we cannot think of the infinite myriad of possibilities available in the field of vibrations that creates and re-creates everything.

Take time to internalize and process each time you do this journey. Write down all of your thoughts and feelings about the experience so that you can observe what shifts for you.

Process Questions

➻ What was it like to experience the formless field of vibration that creates all matter?

➻ What else did you learn from this journey?

➻ What thoughts and feelings are shifting as a result of this experience?

➻ How do you think that visiting the Radiant Field of Infinite Vibrations has changed your way of viewing your creative energy and your creative power?

TEN

Protecting and Actualizing Your Creative Potential

As a creative person, you need to decide and plan how you spend your time and energy. First, you need to set aside and preserve time for your creativity. Second, you need to decide how you will spend that dedicated creative time. Third, you need to choose how to use your creativity for others.

PRESERVING YOUR CREATIVE TIME

Our daily existence always places demands on us. In my creative life, I've learned that even one demand on a day dedicated to creativity tends to diminish the flow of ideas. Even if the demand comes at the end of the day, it still shuts the process down. Many creative folks need open-ended time when the mind can wander from idea to idea to be fully productive in creative work. I've heard the same thing from several of my writer and artist friends. Something about the creative process requires a certain amount of spacious, uninterrupted time.

I have an agreement with one of my dear writer friends, whom I don't get to see very often. We have agreed that if either of us is immersed in a creative flow on the day we've scheduled a visit, we have full permission to cancel. For both of us a cancellation is a great loss, as we love our times of talking together about the work we're doing.

However, we also know that honoring our creative self is even more vital. We love each other enough that neither one of us wants to take that precious creative time away from the other.

Now I realize what I just shared may sound completely crazy to you. However, learning to put your creative time at or very near the top of your list is important. If a creative person rarely has the time to be with his or her ideas, that person can languish. I'm not being dramatic. Using myself as an example, my partner can attest that I become a short-tempered she bear when I haven't had uninterrupted creative time. The act of shutting down my creative energy creates inner anguish and the feeling that I was robbed of something precious because shutting down creative flow is also shutting down a piece of my vitality.

So needless to say, one of the important things you can learn as a creative is when to say no. Saying no can be tricky to do at first, as you might feel guilty about saying or implementing it, particularly with loved ones. All the societal bugaboos about being selfish or self-absorbed and other admonishments can keep us from claiming our own space-time to exercise our creative energy. However, this is just cultural programming, which is especially directed at women who choose to live a creative life. The misogynous nature of Western culture still devalues women who choose a creative life over a more traditional one. At the least, they are perceived as peculiar and even as social outcasts. Learning to defy that nonsense is a huge step in freeing yourself as a creative person.

To be fully honest, my creativity is my primary life focus. I say this as my creativity is a fundamental aspect of my spirituality. It nourishes me and is the source of unlimited and joyful challenge. It's the place where my mind stretches and the lens through which I see life. Through my creativity, I bring ideas into the world to support transforming it and so much more. For those reasons, putting it first is really an action of radical self-caring that supports self-actualization, as well as my spiritual, personal, and professional fulfillment.

Psychologist Abraham Maslow created a hierarchy of needs, represented as a pyramid with basic needs of food, water, and shelter at the bottom and self-fulfillment, including creativity, at the peak. But in many ways, I think creativity transcends *all* the categories in his pyramid. When I am engaged in creativity, I can happily forget to eat, shiver before I get up to get a sweater, and delay a trip to the bathroom. Eventually, I have to tend to my body, but it is begrudgingly done when I'm really in a groove. The same is true about social interactions. I absolutely loathe being interrupted when I'm on a roll—even by people I love. If I am under the weather, a good creative day will pick me up better than a day of rest. I also find that there is absolutely nothing as enriching to my well-being as a great day in the studio.

Finding ways to carve out time to imagine, think, and create can be a real challenge. For instance, my dear partner has learned not to disturb me when I'm just staring out a window, as that is typically a time that I am working through an idea. Of course, on the outside it looks like I'm just vegging out, so I had to explain what I was doing. Nearly every morning, I allow myself time to mentally wander and typically do it in two segments: right after I wake up, while I'm still in bed, and again as I'm getting dressed. I lay out my clothes the night before so I can put everything on without engaging my linear mind and then, while sitting on the bed, I let my mind bubble up ideas and spend some time playing with them. By the time I'm ready to go downstairs, I've had a full creative-thinking session.

What follows is a journey exercise to exorcise the self-sabotaging programming that interferes with putting you and your creativity first.

⟫➤ Removing Self-Sabotaging Programming

For this exercise, you will need:

- A comfortable place to sit, lie down, or move safely
- Your sketch/notebook and a pen
- A clear question you have written down in your sketch/notebook
- A blindfold or bandanna for covering your eyes
- A way to listen to your shamanic journey rhythm recording
- Your post-journey snack and water

Making the Journey

1. Begin your journey in your special place in the Middle World.
2. Call your power animal to you.
3. Greet it, and state your intent: "Take me to a teacher who can remove the self-sabotaging programming I received from my family and culture."
4. Merge with your power animal, and allow it to guide you to the appropriate teacher.
5. Once you arrive at a teacher, ask, "Are you my teacher for this journey?" If you receive an affirmative answer, then state, "Thank you for removing the self-sabotaging program that interferes with my putting my creative self first."
6. With your senses, receive the healing, information, and wisdom the teacher imparts.
7. Continue with the journey until the callback.
8. When you hear the drumming change to the callback signal, thank the teacher, retrace your steps to pass back through the boundary into the Middle World, and return fully to your starting place and ordinary reality.
9. When the callback is finished, take a deep breath, and thank your power animal for this new experience. Open your eyes.
10. Take time to internalize and process what you experienced. Write down all of your thoughts and feelings about the experience.

Process Questions

- ❧ What was it like to receive the healing from the teacher?
- ❧ What else did you learn from this experience?
- ❧ How do you think that this journey will change your way of thinking about the things that you deal with today?

SPENDING YOUR TIME WISELY

We all have demands on our time, and these demands can quickly overwhelm us and take away from our creative time. But with some thought and care, you can manage the time-sucking aspects of your life and preserve your creative time. What follows are a series of suggestions:

- **Domestic partners and children:** Allot specific times with your significant others, and make it quality time. In my life, I talk and hang with my love usually in the evening after supper is cleared away or over breakfast in the morning. We usually dedicate two or three hours each weekday to "us time."
- **Laundry:** You can do the laundry while doing something else, so almost no creative time is lost. If you're a city dweller, you can send out your laundry, which I did when I was single and didn't have a washer and dryer.
- **Cooking:** When it comes to cooking, I prefer to adhere to my friend Heather's dictum: "cook once, eat a bunch." Cook a roast or a big pot of chili or some other large dish that can cover lots of mealtimes in the week. Having the occasional take-out dinner, perhaps once a week, can also help. I've found the mix of two-quarters home-cooked meals, one-quarter pre-prepared food from the natural food store, and one-quarter of takeout to be a good monthly balance to shoot for.
- **Errand day:** I pick one day a week to grocery shop, along with a bunch of other errands, such as stops at the post office, the dry cleaner, the garden center, and a myriad of other possibilities. Errand day can be exhausting, but in the end, it's a lot more efficient to accomplish this all in one day instead of spreading it out piecemeal over several days. I also carefully plan errand day so that everything can be accomplished in one fuel- and time-efficient loop, with no backtracking.

Minimize Screen Time

Nearly everyone in today's world loses a great deal of potential creative time to internet communication. A 2019 article compiling research from over twenty tech-watch sites found that the internet user of today spends an average of *two hours and twenty-two minutes a day* socializing online![1] When I read that statistic, I was frankly horrified. Most of that time is spent on Facebook, Facebook Messenger, Twitter, Instagram, YouTube, and WhatsApp. If you add email to that, you may be looking at close to three or more hours a day!

While I have to use social media as a part of our business, I keep it to twenty to twenty-five minutes a day. I go in, post, browse the notifications, and handle the ones that pertain to my classes first. As I also have a Twitter account, I use programs that link my social applications, which also saves me a lot of time. Email time is kept short, too, and I can usually keep it to thirty- to thirty-five minutes. I go through and respond to urgent ones and ones that pertain to interacting with apprentices, scheduling issues, and speaking engagements and file the others for later.

Working for Others

Another instance when you might want to say no is using your creative energy in ways that don't honor or enhance your own energy. I can't tell you how many times, especially in my very early career as an illustrator, I was offered jobs that just weren't right. Some were either jobs that someone else rejected or ones for clients who said, "I can't pay you, but the job would be great exposure for you!"

There were also clients that honestly didn't respect the time and effort that went into the work. Then there were the jobs that meant using my skills for something I didn't believe in. While I was encouraged to take these assignments both by my wallet and by those around me, I was miserably unhappy both during the process and afterward. Since I was only in my middle teens when I started working, I took some of these jobs. However, after only a very few of them, I learned the importance of saying no. At that point I realized that my efforts needed to be met with reciprocity. This could take the form of full payment or some other equally valuable exchange. In so doing, I also learned to not compromise myself or my worth. Ever.

Social Obligations

There are other nos that you may want to cultivate. These include choosing not to spend time with people who don't nurture you or energetically reciprocate. These are people who take more than they give, such as someone who only calls on you when he or she needs something. That isn't a healthy relationship. If you are being sapped in an exchange, it may be wise to limit or even stop it completely. Of course, some cases are unavoidable, such as taking care of a sick or elderly family member. We are obligated to care for loved ones, but even caretaking needs to be balanced with good self-care and time away to preserve and replenish your energy.

Then there are events such as parties, meetings, or other gatherings. I'm sure there are few among us who haven't lost irreplaceable time to a uselessly meandering meeting, a pointless conversation, or a draining social interaction. Social outings that don't provide a balance of energy for you are ones you may want to think about avoiding. This may sound selfish; however, spending time at an event feeling miserable, resentful, or trapped isn't good for your well-being.

As much as possible, limit obligations that aren't nourishing or that sap your energy, reduce your time-wasting activities, and pull the plug on your draining social engagements. Then spend your precious moments of time on those activities that enrich and renew you. Do these adjustments to your schedule for the purposes of not only preserving your delicious creative time but for your health as well. Oh, and also remember that you're worth it!

To paraphrase U.S. Representative Maxine Waters's famous retort to a rambling witness trying to run down the clock in a congressional inquiry: You'll be "reclaiming *your* time!"

 Turning a No into a Yes for You

For this exercise you will need:

- Your sketch/notebook
- Scissors

- A bunch of letter *n*'s and letter *o*'s cut from newspaper headlines
- A glue stick
- A set of fine-point colored markers

1. Open your book to a spot where clean left and right pages face each other.
2. Lay out all your newspaper letters, and use your glue stick to paste a bunch of nos on the left-hand page. Do your best to fill the entire page with large and small nos. If your page now looks like a crazy ransom note, that's perfect. After all, a well-placed *no!* sets you free from being a hostage to time-sucking obligations.
3. On the blank right-hand page, use your markers to create a colorful page covered with the phrase *yes, for me!* Make the words fun by using different sizes, a fancy font, or embellishing them with lots of color. The idea of this page is to express the joyful effect of saying no to those people and things that impinge on your creative energy.
4. When you're done, if you feel like adding more positive phrases, turn the page and have at it.

A ceremonial exercise like this can really speak volumes to your subconscious. In this exercise, you are able to play with the word *no* to make it much more comfortable to feel inside and to say aloud. In addition, your celebratory *yes* page reminds your subconscious that you are worth taking care of and having time for yourself and that your inherent creative energy is something to really stand up for. Using a playful ceremony like this is a wonderful way to continue reprogramming your subconscious, which is the consciousness that creates your reality. As that aspect of you changes, so does your life. Keep adding messages in creative ways that you invent, and use them to alter your perceptions about what is possible for you to experience.

Once you have completed the exercise, notice how you feel about what you experienced during and after the exercise. Let yourself visualize different situations where you can practice saying no in order to say yes to you and your creative time. Record all you have noticed about your process and may have learned in your sketch/notebook.

Process Questions

- ➡ How did it feel to say no?
- ➡ What occurred inside and around you when you made the choice to preserve your creative time?
- ➡ How did it feel doing the "Turning a No into a Yes for You" exercise?
- ➡ What other ways do you think saying no will provide you with a big yes in your life?

99 PERCENT PERSPIRATION: ACTUALIZING YOUR CREATIVE POTENTIAL

We've done a lot of exploring over the course of these pages. We've explored what creativity is, how its flow is influenced by feeling, how you can find your own creative rhythms, how to get unstuck, and what the role of expanded consciousness is. What still needs to be said is how to actualize your creative energy through expressing it.

Thomas Edison was credited with the idea that "Genius is one percent inspiration and 99 percent perspiration"; however, the American essayist, author, and lecturer Kate Sanborn stated that "genius is inspiration, talent and perspiration." In either case, it is clear that along with cultivating inspiration and the expansion of your creative energy, you are also going to have to put in effort to express your creativity.

What follows are some time-tested methods to keep the creative taps flowing.

Journey Forth

Practice the journey exercises in this book to keep your creative mind supple and well muscled. Since journeying is also imaginative, you will be giving your mind a time to dream and play. Go on shamanic journeys to meet your muse as you might a human mentor. Make sure you listen to the drumming as you journey, as that rhythm will assist in the rewiring upgrade of your brain and *always* return fully to ordinary reality.

Make a commitment to journey at least once a week. I guarantee if you keep writing down things you are curious about you and journey about them, you will get far more interesting information and experiences than you would from passively listening to the virtual assistant in your phone or smart home device. Journeying will rewire your brain, boost your creative energy, and irrevocably transform you in many positive ways. Always remember it is only here in our ordinary reality world that you will experience the changes the journeys produce. That is why coming fully back and grounding after a journey is so crucial.

Work with Your Creative Energy Every Single Day—No Exceptions

It is important to return to the exercises in this book to keep engaging your creative nature. If those exercises start to feel boring or stale, make up variations and have fun with them. Spend time putting down ideas that come to you upon waking or falling asleep. Capture images and things that stimulate ideas in your sketch/notebook. Make your creativity a living thread in your life.

I have an artist friend who took care of her husband who had a progressive motor neuron disease. Caring for him took up all of her day, and she took many hundreds more steps in those days than any time before he became ill. During this time, she couldn't go down to her studio to work as she couldn't hear if her husband needed her while in that room. Undaunted, she found another brilliant way to exercise her creativity. Each day, she'd put a bit of colored, unspun wool in her shoes. At the end of the day, the many steps she had taken compressed the wool into felt. She cut that felt into a heart and mounted it to a panel that she passed dozens of times a day. This was a concrete expression of the fact that the steps and exhaustion she felt were manifestations of her love. When the panel was full, she began giving the felt hearts to friends and family who brought meals and offered support. In this way, her creativity connected her entire community of helpers while lightening her heart during a very difficult period.

Shoot for Volume, Not Perfection

The efforts you make exercising your creative mind are never wasted. I often say that *every* idea I have ever had got turned into something useful. That is even the case when the idea wasn't right for the original purpose or simply didn't pan out. That is because ideas always beget new ones, so keeping them in your sketch/notebook is always a good practice. Without allowing any inhibiting thoughts to arise, think about ways things could be improved; dream up a new solution even if it seems impractical. Remember, Leonardo da Vinci drew plans for planes, tanks, and helicopters long before the technology was available to produce them. The idea is to keep having ideas so that they flow more and more easily. They don't have to be good or practical ideas; let even your craziest ideas take flight, and capture them in your sketch/notebook. The more ideas you have, the more ideas you will generate until you become an idea machine.

Steal Ideas

One of my art school instructors once told me that there are no original ideas. He added that every perceived new idea was built on something that came before. For instance, every color, texture, and line has already been expressed in nature. They become unique through the unique perspective of each artist, author, or other creative person who interprets those expressions in their own way from the perspective of their own life, culture, and inner world. I'm not suggesting copying someone else's ideas but allowing yourself to be inspired by others' works by observing and preserving them as creative fodder.

Toward that end, every artist I've known has some kind of "swipe file." In the old days, that was a file cabinet filled with pictures for reference. Today, it might be your Pinterest or Instagram account. Keep images of things that stimulate your senses, photos of nature, other people's artistic expressions, and anything else that fills you with inspiration.

Another trick is to read a lot. Creativity is stimulated by others' words and ideas. Read good speculative fiction to spend time in another world with different parameters. Spend time in a bookstore or library browsing colorful children's books. Read nonfiction to keep learning something new about a variety of different subjects. Fill your brain as if it were a limitless container, and you may be surprised by what creative ideas eventually spill forth.

If you have a living creative role model, learn all you can about how that person solves problems. Get in his or her head and think about how you might follow a similar cognitive and creative path. It's a real delight seeing how other creative minds work. Everyone does things a bit differently, so you can learn new ways of approaching a problem or learn new solutions by spending time with other creative thinkers.

Conscious Learning

Choose a topic that you are curious about, and learn everything you can about it. You might choose to study a new language, as it will teach you a boatload about your own native language, how people communicate, and how different languages are intimately woven into the culture that begets them.

You might choose to take a class in home maintenance. It is a great way to learn another way to problem-solve and develop more eye-hand coordination. At the very least, you'll be able to fix the little things around the house, saving yourself some money.

Get a set of good binoculars, and start learning about the animals and birds that visit your home. Notice their habits, how they live, and when they show up at the feeder; in the process, you will develop a new set of observational skills.

If you have an immigrant community in your area, visit it, and begin to learn about the culture of those that live there. Taste their food and find ways that you can support their community and learn about their customs. Be curious, and let the community guide your path so that you don't impose your ideas but rather learn their ways of understanding the world with true respect and caring.

Learn to play a musical instrument. Although I had played guitar in a party band when I was young, I decided to learn Scottish fiddling in my late fifties, just for the hell of it. I spent a few years learning and practicing, eventually getting fairly skilled at playing at a dozen or so spritely Scottish tunes. The mental challenge of being a rank beginner at something again created lots of new pathways in my brain, and I had a ball doing it. (Now, I have my sights set on acquiring and playing a Viking-age *tagelharpa,* but that's a story for another time!)

Rest and Put a Project Aside for a While

I usually have several projects going at once. This allows me to put one aside when it isn't flowing and to pick up another to refresh my creative mind. More often than not, they are very different kinds of projects. They might be a book and an article or as different as a book and a piece of silversmithing or some other object I've had an idea about making.

Truthfully, I attend to feeding my creative mind every chance I can. That might mean taking a walk by the river; listening to a podcast on a topic I'm curious about; visiting a beautiful, wild place; trying a new activity; or spending time with interesting people who offer a different perspective on life. All of them rest my mind from a current challenge yet keep the creativity engine quietly humming.

If those choices don't provide the needed restoration, I might quietly browse images or listen to a new piece of music. What is important is to find ways to rest and refresh yourself without going blank. While electronic entertainment such as TV, Netflix, and the like can be fun, beware of passively vegging out. Going numb isn't resting; it's shutting down and will dampen your creativity.

Get Feedback

Develop connections with other people who are creative, and best of all, seek those who are even more creative than you are. Support each other to exchange ideas. Make the session mutual, and agree to be clear but also respectful in your critiques. When asked, honestly share your perspective on others' work, and allow your work to be critiqued, too.

Don't be afraid to show your ideas. Develop a thick skin and a positive attitude. When you're on the receiving end, remember to be courageous about hearing others' input without feeling wounded and to be willing to rework your ideas to incorporate valid comments. Clearheaded, honest feedback is vital. This is a great way to not go around in mental circles on a project or become insular in your ideas. Others may actually have useful points about how you could better express what you're thinking about. You don't have to agree; you just have to listen and ask yourself how that perspective might alter a direction or improve an idea.

Create What You Love

If you love flowers, then by all means immerse yourself in them—their colors, scents, textures, habits, how they make you feel, who developed a particular variety, and so on. Then let that fuel your creativity. Perhaps you might learn to do watercolor or photography to capture how they look in the morning dew. Maybe you want to learn the science of scent to create your own fragrances. Perhaps you might develop a new "crazy idea" for a garden layout. My point is that as you connect your love of something to your creativity, you are supporting your passion by more deeply immersing yourself in what you love.

Finding ways to add more of what you love in your life is not only satisfying but also fills your life with more joy, beauty, and meaning. For instance, one of my power animals takes the form of a polar bear. It is a spirit that I love and has given me so much over the years. I honor this spirit every day, and I have even been blessed to see polar bears in ordinary reality. The experience of being close to them in their natural habitat was a lifelong dream and a life-changing experience. It deepened my love and commitment to my helping spirit far beyond what I thought was possible and also strengthened the connections I have to his earthly kin. As a way to honor this spirit companion, I wear a necklace dedicated to him that I crafted from silver. All around my home, I have painted images of bears and the others in my cadre of spiritual support. I consider these images one way to honor my helping spirits. Engaging my creativity around my power animals and the others of my tutelary spirits helps to bridge my ordinary life with the nonordinary world of the spirits. In essence, by using my creativity, I have woven the tangible and intangible into a seamless fabric.

CONCLUSION

A New Paradigm of Creativity

As caring, creative people, you and I can help to make sure that future generations have a healthy world in which to flourish and grow. This book is meant as a support for you to awaken your crazy wisdom, express your amazing talents, and be deliciously creative. It is my goal to inspire your heart, nurture your hope, give you courage, and offer you the best shot at being the imaginative and energetic being that you were born to be.

How we choose to use our energy affects the world around us, as we are hardwired into the collective. As each of us awakens our full potential, we participate in the awakening of our entire species. Remember, a very small number of people living in a new, healthy, and creative way can create a metaparadigm. Just 8,944 people with their creative energy on full power can help to radically transform the present and set us on a new course for our future. We have the creativity as a species to not only create new technology but to also completely reinvent ourselves. We can reimagine being sustainable and participating in the restoration of nature. Once dreamed, we can harness our creativity to make it a reality.

Let's go!

RESOURCES

Creative Organizations and Supplies

WEBSITES AND ORGANIZATIONS

HeartMath Institute (www.heartmath.com): Research institute for helping people to reduce stress and experience increased peace, satisfaction, and enjoyment

Inner Traditions (audio.innertraditions.com/shacre): Visit the publisher's website to access the book's three audio tracks: "Tapping into the Creative Energy in and around You," "Repairing Your Energy after Experiencing Fear or Anger," and "Shamanic Journey Drumming."

ShamanicTeachers.com: A website for finding shamanic teachers and practitioners worldwide

Spirit Passages (www.spiritpassages.com): The author's website with information about workshops and individual shamanic healing sessions

INSPIRATIONAL PERIODICALS AND BLOGS

Beautiful Bizarre: Art, Culture, Couture (https://beautifulbizarre.net): Contemporary art magazine

Chapel of the Sacred Mirror (www.cosm.org): Art of Alex Grey

Colossal (www.thisiscolossal.com): International platform for contemporary art and visual expression

Hi-Fructose (https://hifructose.com): Contemporary art magazine

Myth & Moor (www.terriwindling.com/blog): Writer, editor, and artist Terri Windling's blog

Sacred Hoop: Celebrating the Circle of Life (www.sacredhoop.org): International magazine about shamanism, sacred wisdom, and earth spirituality

CHOOSING THE RIGHT SKETCH/NOTEBOOK

When shopping for a sketchbook, there are a few things to consider.

First, try to avoid buying a cheap book at a chain craft store. I know that might sound elitist, but nothing is worse than a sketchbook with a cover that bends, loosens, or frays and pages that weaken from erasure, allow bleed-through from one page to the next, or simply fall apart from use. Your precious creativity demands a great receptacle.

First thing to consider is binding. You can have either sewn or spiral binding. Both have advantages and disadvantages. A sewn binding can sometimes limit how far you can open the book flat, although some sewn bindings compensate for that and books are able to lie nearly flat. A spiral binding will always lie perfectly flat; however, with extended use, the pages can become worn where they meet the spiral binding and tear loose. Whichever binding you choose, the pages can be bound either on the side or at the top, giving either a portrait- or landscape-oriented surface for your efforts.

Next you need to consider covers, either hard or soft. I like a hard cover as it feels substantial, but a soft cover makes it easier to stuff the book in a pocket.

Then there is the paper. You can choose paper with a *cold-plate finish,* which has a lot of tooth or texture and is great for pastels, graphite pencils, and charcoal; a *vellum finish,* which is smooth and good for ink as well as pencil; or a *hot-plate finish,* which is extremely smooth and best for harder pencils, pen and ink, and technical pens such as the Rapidograph. Some books have papers that can withstand wet media, such as watercolor. Colors vary as well, from different shades of white to gray and tan. I always look for a bright white paper; however, you may prefer a more off-white ivory paper, found in Moleskine sketchbooks. Darker-tinted papers may be found in the Hahnemühle sketchbook line, which has books with white, gray, or cappuccino paper, and the Strathmore 400 Series Toned Sketch Hardbound Art Journals, which have either cool gray or warm tan paper.

Art supplies stores offer a huge range of different sketchbooks to satisfy just about any need. You can find Moleskine, Hahnemühle, Canson, Art Alternatives, Stillman & Birn Alpha Series Sketchbooks, and others, depending on the shop.

Finally, you may (like me) want a book that either has its own band to keep it closed or fits inside a canvas or leather folio with a pocket. A band can keep loose papers from falling out, and a pouch or pocket can hold a sharpener, eraser, and other necessities.

CHOOSING THE RIGHT CREATIVE IMPLEMENTS

As with the sketchbook, you mustn't skimp on the materials you use in them, either.

Likely, you were told to bring a number 2 pencil to school for taking standardized tests; however, pencils have many levels of hardness and quality. The numbers range from 8B, which is the softest lead, to 6H, which is the hardest. The middle grade of hardness is HB, and that old test pencil is a 2B.

My personal favorite pencil is the Palomino Blackwing 602, as it delivers a smooth dark line with graphite that is hard enough to hold a sharp point. The density of the graphite is also consistent for the pencil's entire length. I care about that because the graphite in many pencils can be quite inconsistent, so that a smooth line suddenly gets scratchy. I also like to use Derwent, Faber-Castell, and Staedtler pencils. If you're fond

My favorite pencil.

of using a soft pencil with really smooth, jet-black graphite, you might want to try the Prismacolor Premier Ebony Graphite Sketching Pencil.

In colored pencils, there are lots of choices. If you are looking for a very good, versatile set, choose the Prismacolor Premier line. They have a waxy consistency and are somewhat inconsistent in their overall quality but offer the best range of colors for the best price. If you love colored pencils, you may want to splurge on a set of the very fine Faber-Castell Polychromos series or the Faber-Castell Albrecht Dürer Artist's Watercolor Pencil set. Of course, if you have hit the lottery, got that promised bequest from your rich uncle, or simple have money to burn, you may want *both* sets in their luscious, ridiculously expensive, limited-edition Faber-Castell KARLBOX set that also contains fine pastels, pencils, pens, sharpeners, and erasers and is housed in a case designed by Karl Lagerfeld.

For India ink, the best choice for over 140 years is Higgins Black Magic Waterproof Ink. For those who like to draw with a dip pen, this is the best choice. With a dip pen, you can make a line that varies with pressure and so bring a sensual quality to drawings that rivals the brush. Not surprisingly, writers and artists have been using dip pens for a very long time. If you are so inclined, get a comfortable handle that will take a variety of drawing nibs. The steel nibs, or points that contact the paper, come in an incredible variety. The company that has the widest variety of reliable dip pens is Speedball, which has been in business for over a century. Browsing the company website will give you insights into the wide world of this ancient and dependable drawing, lettering, and ruling tool.

For some, having a flexible line is irrelevant in that they use very fine, consistent pen strokes or dots layered over each other to produce their work. My illustrations are done in this way. I prefer to use a technical pen, such as the Koh-I-Noor Rapidograph, with its reservoir filled with Koh-I-Noor Rapidograph Ultradraw Waterproof Ink and tipped by a very fine 3x0 nib. I use it on vellum paper or illustration board, as long as it has an ultrasmooth, hot-press finish.

For colored inks that you can use in a technical pen, or with a dip pen or brush, you can choose waterproof varieties such as Higgins Waterproof Drawing Inks or Dr. Ph. Martin's Bombay India Inks. For liquid colors that can be worked again after drying (in other words, not waterproof), you may choose Dr. Ph. Martin's Radiant Concentrated Water Color sets.

Last, if you want to completely forgo filling a pen or brush with ink, there are several excellent pigment pens available. These utilize a waterproof archival ink that rivals Higgins Black Magic; however, they are housed in plastic barrels and are, sadly, disposable. However, if you work outdoors or in situations where refilling your pen with an open bottle of ink isn't an option, you may want to try them. For those situations, I've found the Pigma Micron by Sakura is quite satisfactory. The pens are available in several thicknesses and a few different colors. The black is rich and satiny and reproduces very well.

If you want to work with more color, you may want to get a small, portable watercolor set. Winsor & Newton offers several exceptionally useful versions containing replaceable, twelve to twenty-four half-cakes of color and a small, integrated mixing palette to blend colors together. The sets include a half-sized number 5 brush made from blended synthetic fibers, and some sets also have a small water bottle and sponge. Some companies are now offering synthetic fiber brushes that have a water reservoir in the handle. Arteza sets offer this option and come in varieties with as many as thirty-six colors.

OK, now I have to discuss brushes. I prefer to use Winsor & Newton Series 7 Kolinsky Sable Miniature Round Brushes for watercolor, ink, and acrylic paint. I love their feel, the way they lay down color, the resiliency of the hairs returning to shape after a stroke, and how long they can last—when properly cared for. As I tend to use mostly small, fine brushes, I have found that synthetics can't deliver the same performance. However, true Kolinsky sable brushes are terribly expensive, especially in larger sizes, and though they can last a very long time with care, eventually even the best loved of them will need to be replaced.

Recently, I have heard some buzz about the Mimik Kolinsky Sable Mini Deluxe Travel Brush Set for watercolor work. As the name implies, they mimic natural sable but have animal-friendly synthetic "hairs." They are handmade in Germany and have a protective chrome cap that, once removed from the head of the brush, can be added to the back to extend the handle. The set comes with sizes #4, #6, #8, and #12. I haven't yet tried them, but you may want to check them out, as they get good reviews, and the whole kit costs quite a bit less than a single #12 natural Kolinsky sable brush.

ART SUPPLIES STORES

If at all possible, even if you have to travel to a larger city, give yourself the treat of going to a really good art supplies store. The chain stores that carry some art supplies along with craft materials are OK in a pinch, but if you want to experience the full range of products that are available, you need to go to a brick-and-mortar art supplies store. There, you can experience a wide variety of sketchbooks, drawing and writing materials, and media. Handling a product and hearing from the experienced artists in the shop will help you to make informed choices.

Many also carry art books and a wide variety of containers to carry tools and finished work, as well as slick new products that you may want to try. The local art supplies store is also a great place to meet other people expressing their creativity. In our local shop, you can run into the famous as well as the beginner, and the staff is wonderful at helping the customer to find the right solutions.

If you have a local store, please purchase materials from that store to keep it in business. However, if you have no other option, these are excellent online stores to check out:

The Artist and Craftsman
(www.artistcraftsman.com)

The Artist and Craftsman originated in Maine and now has stores across the United States, as well as a fine online presence. If you love painting on wood panels, it has the best choice of good but inexpensive painting panels on the market, as well as a full range of other fine supplies. If you're ever in Portland, Maine, check out the fabulously funky flagship store!

The Art Mart
(http://fineart.artmartmaine.com/defaultframe.asp)

A small store with an online presence that offers great prices. They specialize in catering to students at the Maine College of Art and also have an online presence.

Dick Blick
(www.dickblick.com)

For sheer volume and variety, you can't beat this online company. My old standby was Pearl Paint in New York City, but since it's gone, Dick Blick has become my go-to online supplier for hard-to-find goodies. They carry a huge range of different sketchbooks to satisfy just about any need. You can find Moleskine, Hahnemühle, Canson, Stillman & Birn Alpha Series Sketchbooks, and others.

Jerry's Artarama
(www.jerrysartarama.com)

Jerry's Artarama carries Reflexions Watercolor Journals. These are spiral-bound, multimedia books that have acid-free, cold-press paper and an elastic band to hold the book closed.

Notes

INTRODUCTION:
THE POWER OF CREATIVE ENERGY

1. Toynbee, "Has America Neglected Her Creative Minority?," 8.

CHAPTER 1. HOW SHAMANIC CREATIVITY
SUPPORTS WHOLENESS

1. Pearce in Blackie, *If Women Rose Rooted,* 195.
2. Wallas, *The Art of Thought.*
3. Parry, "Exaptation."
4. Bounds, "How Handwriting Trains the Brain."

CHAPTER 2. FEELINGS: THE DANCE OF
DISSONANCE AND HARMONY

1. McCraty, *Science of the Heart.*
2. Lipton, "Change Your Thoughts."
3. This was shared by HeartMath staff member Deborah Rozman during a presentation at the Conference on Science and Consciousness in Albuquerque, New Mexico, in 2001 and reiterated by Gregg Braden in his presentation at the same conference.
4. Williamson, *A Return to Love.*
5. Lipton, "4 Ways to Change Your Thoughts."

CHAPTER 3. NURTURING YOUR CREATIVE BRAIN

1. Reid, "How Neuroscientist Michael Grybko Defines Creativity."
2. Reber, "What Is the Memory Capacity of the Human Brain?"

3. Andreasen, "A Journey into Chaos: Creativity and the Unconscious."

4. Comings, "The New Physics of Space, Time and Light."

5. Comings, "The New Physics of Space, Time and Light."

6. Stancák and Kuna, "EEG Changes during Forced Alternate Nostril Breathing."

7. André, "Proper Breathing Brings Better Health."

CHAPTER 4. ALTERED STATES AND CREATIVITY

1. Bourguignon, "Introduction."

2. This interview took place at the Chapel of Sacred Mirrors Visionary Salon in 2013.

3. Bateson, *Steps to an Ecology of Mind,* 306.

4. Saniotis and Henneberg, "An Evolutionary Approach Toward Exploring Altered States of Consciousness."

5. From the artist's website, www.alexgrey.com/media/writing/essays /the-creative-process-and-entheogens.

6. Schartner et al., "Increased Spontaneous MEG Signal Diversity."

7. Metzner, "Consciousness Expansion and Counterculture," 17.

8. Vitebsky, *The Shaman,* 14.

9. Metzner, "Consciousness Expansion and Counterculture," 17–18.

CHAPTER 5. SHAMANIC JOURNEYING TO THE LOWER AND UPPER WORLDS

1. McKenna, "Opening the Doors of Creativity."

2. Hoppe, "Psychoanalysis, Hemispheric Specialization, and Creativity."

3. Devlet, "Rock Art and the Material Culture," in ed. Neil Price, *The Archaeology of Shamanism,* 45.

4. Metzner, "Consciousness Expansion and Counterculture."

5. Harner, *The Way of the Shaman,* 53.

6. Fischer et al., "The Ancestor Effect."

CHAPTER 6. SHAMANIC JOURNEYING INTO UNKNOWN TERRITORY

1. Kowalewski, "Metaphysical Tracking."

2. Speck, *Neskapi,* 160.

CHAPTER 7. THE EBB AND FLOW OF CREATIVE ENERGY

1. Thompson, "Priming Your Subconscious for Creativity."

2. Mehta, Zhu, and Cheema, "Is Noise Always Bad?"

3. Atchley, Strayer, and Atchley, "Creativity in the Wild."

CHAPTER 8. BUILDING THE IMAGINATION

1. Bariso, "There Are Actually 3 Types of Empathy."

2. Van Hiel et al., "The Relationship between Emotional Abilities."

3. Wickelgreen, "How Do You Spot a Genius?"

CHAPTER 9. EMBRACING YOUR HIGHEST CONSCIOUSNESS

1. Glattfelder, *Information–Consciousness–Reality.*

2. Laszlo, *Science and the Reenchantment of the Cosmos.*

3. Comings, "The Quantum Plenum."

CHAPTER 10. PROTECTING AND ACTUALIZING YOUR CREATIVE POTENTIAL

1. Georgiev, "How Much Time Do People Spend on Social Media in 2021?"

Bibliography

André, Christophe. "Proper Breathing Brings Better Health." *Scientific American,* January 15, 2019.

Andreasen, N. C. "A Journey into Chaos: Creativity and the Unconscious." In ed. A. R. Singh and S. A. Sigh, *Brain, Mind and Consciousness: An International, Interdisciplinary Perspective,* 42–53. Mumbai, India: Medknow, 2011.

Atchley R. A., D. L. Strayer, and P. Atchley. "Creativity in the Wild: Improving Creative Reasoning through Immersion in Natural Settings." *PLoS ONE* 7, no. 12 (2012): e51474.

Bariso, Justin. "There Are Actually 3 Types of Empathy. Here's How They Differ—and How You Can Develop Them All." Inc. (website), September 19, 2019.

Bateson, Gregory. "The Logical Categories of Learning and Communication." In *Steps to an Ecology of Mind*, 279–308. Chicago: University of Chicago Press, 1972.

Blackie, Sharon. *If Women Rose Rooted: The Journey to Authenticity and Belonging.* Kent, UK: September, 2016.

Bounds, Gwendolyn. "How Handwriting Trains the Brain: Forming Letters Is Key to Learning, Memory, Ideas." *Wall Street Journal*, October 5, 2010.

Bourguignon, Erika. "Introduction: A Framework for the Comparative Study of Altered States of Consciousness." In ed. E. Bourguignon, *Religion, Altered States of Consciousness and Social Change*, 3–33. Columbus: Ohio State University, 1973.

Comings, Mark. "The New Physics of Space, Time and Light." Keynote address, 2005 True North Annual Conference. Portland, Maine, 2005.

———. "The Quantum Plenum: The Hidden Key to Life, Energetics and Sentience." ISSSEEM conference. *Bridges* 17, no. 1 (Spring 2006): 4–20.

Czaplicka, M. A. *Aboriginal Siberia, A Study in Social Anthropology.* London: Oxford University Press, 1969. First published 1914.

Fischer, P., A. Sauer, C. Vogrincic, and S. Weisweiler. "The Ancestor Effect: Thinking about Our Genetic Origin Enhances Intellectual Performance." *European Journal of Social Psychology* 41 (2011): 11–16.

Flor-Henry, Pierre, Yakov Shapiro, and Corine Sombrun. "Brain Changes during a Shamanic Trance: Altered Modes of Consciousness, Hemispheric Laterality, and Systemic Psychobiology." *Cogent Psychology* 4, no. 1 (2017).

Georgiev, Deyan. "How Much Time Do People Spend on Social Media in 2021?" Techjury (website), March 29, 2021.

Glattfelder, James B. *Information—Consciousness—Reality: How a New Understanding of the Universe Can Help Answer Age-Old Questions of Existence.* Frontiers Collection. Cham, Switzerland: Springer Open, 2019.

Goswami, Amit. *Quantum Creativity.* Carlsbad, Calif.: Hay House, 2014.

Grey, Alex. *Transfigurations.* Rochester, Vt.: Inner Traditions International, 2001.

Halifax, Joan. *Shaman: The Wounded Healer.* London: Thames Hudson, 1992.

———. *Shamanic Voices: A Survey of Visionary Narratives.* New York: E. P. Dutton, 1979.

Harner, Michael. *The Way of the Shaman.* New York: HarperCollins Publishers, 1990.

Harner, Sandra. "Shamanism and the Immune Response." The Frontiers of Consciousness Lecture Series. Institute of Noetic Science; San Francisco, June 26, 2002. From a CD recording of the lecture produced by the Foundation for Shamanic Studies, Mill Valley, Calif., 2002.

Harner, Sandra, and Warren W. Tryon. "Psychological and Immunological Responses to Shamanic Journeying with Drumming." *Shaman* 4, nos. 1–2 (1996): 89–97.

Hawkins, David R. *Power vs Force: The Hidden Determinants of Human Behavior.* Carlsbad, Calif.: Hay House, 1995 (2002 edition).

Hoppe, Klaus D. "Psychoanalysis, Hemispheric Specialization, and Creativity." *Journal of the American Academy of Psychoanalysis* 17, no. 2 (1989): 253–69.

Johnson, Stephen. *Where Good Ideas Come from: The Natural History of Innovation.* New York: Riverbend Books, 2010.

Koestler, Arthur. *The Act of Creation: A Study of the Conscious and Unconscious*

Processes in Humor, Scientific Discovery and Art. New York: Macmillan, 1964.

Kowalewski, D. "Metaphysical Tracking: The Oldest Ecopsychology." *International Journal of Transpersonal Studies* 23 (2004): 65–74.

Laszlo, Ervin. *Science and the Reenchantment of the Cosmos: The Rise of the Integral Vision of Reality*. New York: Simon and Schuster, 2006.

Lipton, Bruce H. "Change Your Thoughts: Change Everything." YouTube video. Uploaded Aug. 26, 2019 by Team Fearless.

———. "4 Ways to Change Your Thoughts." *Bruce H. Lipton, Ph.D.* (blog), July 12, 2017.

Mack, John E. *Passport to the Cosmos*. New York: Crown/Random House, 1999.

McCraty, Rollin. *Science of the Heart: Exploring the Role of the Heart in Human Performance*. 2 vols. Boulder Creek, Calif.: HeartMath Institute, 2015.

McKenna, Terence. "Opening the Doors of Creativity." Talk, sponsored by Carnegie Museum of Art, Port Hueneme, California, October 20, 1990.

Mehta, Ravi, Rui (Juliet) Zhu, and Amar Cheema. "Is Noise Always Bad? Exploring the Effects of Ambient Noise on Creative Cognition." *Journal of Consumer Research* 39, no. 4 (2012): 784–99.

Metzner, Ralph. "Consciousness Expansion and Counterculture in the 1960s and Beyond." *MAPS Bulletin: Special edition: Psychedelics and Ecology* 19, no. 1 (Spring 2009): 16–20.

Nordby, Jacob. *Blessed Are the Weird: A Manifesto for Creatives*. Boise, Idaho: Manifesto, 2016.

Parry, Wynne. "Exaptation: How Evolution Uses What's Available." Live Science (website), 2014.

Price, Neil, ed. *The Archaeology of Shamanism*. London and New York: Routledge, 2001.

Reber, Paul. "What Is the Memory Capacity of the Human Brain?" *Scientific American,* May 1, 2020.

Reid, Kelton. "How Neuroscientist Michael Grybko Defines Creativity" (podcast). Rainmaker.FM, April 27, 2015.

Rein, Glen, and Rollin McCraty. "Local and Non-Local Effects of Coherent Heart Frequencies on Conformational Changes of DNA," compilation of research done 1981–1993 (Observation equipment: Hewlett Packard UV Absorption Spectrophotometer).

Rysdyk, Evelyn C. *Modern Shamanic Living*. York, Maine: Samuel Weiser, 1999.

————. *A Spirit Walker's Guide to Shamanic Implements*. Newbury, Mass.: RedWheel/Weiser, 2012.

Saniotis, Arthur, and Maciej Henneberg. "An Evolutionary Approach Toward Exploring Altered States of Consciousness, Mind–Body Techniques, and Non-Local Mind." *Journal of New Paradigm Research* 67, no. 3 (2011) 182–200.

Schartner, Michael M., Robin L. Carhart-Harris, Adam B. Barrett, Anil K. Seth, and Suresh D. Muthukumaraswamy. "Increased Spontaneous MEG Signal Diversity for Psychoactive Doses of Ketamine, LSD and Psilocybin." *Scientific Reports* 7 (April 2017).

Schwartz, Gary, and Linda G. S. Russek. *The Living Energy Universe*. Charlottesville, Va.: Hampton Roads, 1999.

Speck, Frank G. *Neskapi: The Savage Hunters of the Labrador Peninsula*. Norman: University of Oklahoma Press, 1935.

Stancák, A. Jr., and M. Kuna. "EEG Changes during Forced Alternate Nostril Breathing." *International Journal of Psychophysiology* 18, no. 1 (October 1994): 75–79.

Talbot, Michael. *The Holographic Universe*. New York: HarperCollins, 1992.

Thompson, Stuart. "Priming Your Subconscious for Creativity." Neuromavin (website), accessed June 11, 2021.

Toynbee, Arnold. "Has America Neglected Her Creative Minority?" *Sooner Magazine,* January 1962: 7–9.

Van Hiel, A., J. De keersmaecker, E. Onraet, T. Haesevoets, A. Roets, and J. R. J. Fontaine. "The Relationship between Emotional Abilities and Right-Wing and Prejudiced Attitudes." *Emotion* 19, no. 5 (2019): 917–22.

Vitebsky, Piers. *The Shaman*. New York: Macmillan, 1995.

Wallas, G. *The Art of Thought*. New York: Harcourt, Brace and World, 1926.

Wardwell, Allen. *Tangible Visions*. New York: Monacelli Press, 1996.

Wickelgreen, Ingrid. "How Do You Spot a Genius?" *Streams of Consciousness* (blog). Scientific American (website), 2012.

Williamson, Marianne. *A Return to Love: Reflections on the Principles of a Course in Miracles*. New York: HarperCollins, 1992.

Index

About the Author

Evelyn C. Rysdyk is an internationally recognized shamanic practitioner and bestselling author whose other titles include *The Norse Shaman, Spirit Walking: A Course in Shamanic Power,* and *A Spirit Walker's Guide to Shamanic Tools* as well as *The Nepalese Shamanic Path* with indigenous Nepali jhankri, Bhola N. Banstola.

Along with her writings, Evelyn is an impassioned teacher and is a featured presenter for many global online programs.

For more than thirty years, Evelyn has delighted in supporting people to remember their sacred place in All That Is. Whether through face-to-face contact with individual clients, through online contact with her students from around the world, or through the printed word, Evelyn uses her loving humor, storytelling, and passion to open people's hearts and inspire them to live more joyful, fulfilling, and purposeful lives. As people awaken their full selves, they are much more likely and able to make their unique contributions toward transforming our world.

Evelyn draws her inspiration from the wild coasts of northern New England, where she continues to manifest all manner of creative mischief.

BOOKS OF RELATED INTEREST

The Norse Shaman
Ancient Spiritual Practices of the Northern Tradition
by Evelyn C. Rysdyk

The Nepalese Shamanic Path
Practices for Negotiating the Spirit World
by Evelyn C. Rysdyk
With Bhola Nath Banstola
Foreword by Sandra Ingerman

Animal Medicine
A Curanderismo Guide to Shapeshifting, Journeying,
and Connecting with Animal Allies
by Erika Buenaflor, M.A., J.D.

Cleansing Rites of Curanderismo
Limpias Espirituales of Ancient Mesoamerican Shamans
by Erika Buenaflor, M.A., J.D.

Speaking with Nature
Awakening to the Deep Wisdom of the Earth
by Sandra Ingerman and Llyn Roberts

Shamanic Mysteries of Peru
The Heart Wisdom of the High Andes
by Vera Lopez and Linda Star Wolf, Ph.D.

Earth Spirit Dreaming
Shamanic Ecotherapy Practices
by Elizabeth E. Meacham, Ph.D.
Foreword by Christopher M. Bache, Ph.D.

The Lost Art of Heart Navigation
A Modern Shaman's Field Manual
by Jeff D. Nixa, J.D., M.Div.

INNER TRADITIONS • BEAR & COMPANY
P.O. Box 388
Rochester, VT 05767
1-800-246-8648
www.InnerTraditions.com

Or contact your local bookseller